JONAS *and* RAQUEL ARRAIS

D0172137

Joys and Challenges of the Pastoral Family

Safeliz

Title: Joys and Challenges of the Pastoral Family
Authors: Jonas and Raquel Arrais

Copyright by © Editorial Safeliz, S. L.

Editorial Safeliz, S. L.
Pradillo, 6 · Pol. Ind. La Mina
E-28770 · Colmenar Viejo, Madrid, Spain
Tel.: [+34] 91 845 98 77 · Fax: [+34] 91 845 98 65
admin@safeliz.com · www.safeliz.com

This book was produced in cooperation with the Ministerial Association
of the General Conference of the Seventh-day Adventist Church.

October 2018: 1ˢᵗ edition

ISBN: 978-84-7208-677-7

PRINTED IN THE EU
IMP11

DEDICATION

To GOD, the source of joy
in all seasons.

To our sons,
Tiago Costa Arrais
Andre Costa Arrais
Who are precious gifts from God,
part of the ministerial team,
and an inspiration to us.

To our daughters in-law,
Paula Leme Arrais
Natalia Nardy Arrais
Who are of great blessings in
our family and support in our
ministerial journey.

To our grand-children,
Benjamin Leme Arrais
Joana Leme Arrais
Noah Nardy Arrais
Who motivate us to live in the
present with joy and face the
future with hope and confidence.

ACKNOWLEDGMENTS

Writing a book is harder than we thought and more rewarding than we could have ever imagined. None of this would have been possible without the support of the General Conference Ministerial Association.

There are also plenty of people who helped bring this book to fruition, and we are grateful to all of them. Once this book started to go from concept in our minds to a manuscript, there were many people involved who deserve to be acknowledged and thanked. Some of them are: John M. Fowler with his excellent suggestions in making this a better book than we ever could have done on our own. Teresita Perez for enabling us to keep the vision of a finished product. Sheryl Beck for her wisdom in shaping this book. Alfredo Garcia-Marenko for his valuable and tireless support in this project. Erika Miike for her wonderful expertise applied to the layout and design. Their ideas, suggestions, and skills helped us get to a manuscript that made us say, "Yes, it's finally a book!" It is because of their efforts and encouragement that we have a contribution to pass on to the worldwide ministerial family.

FOREWORD

Yes, there are many joys and challenges in being called by our Lord to be a pastoral family! We thank and praise Him regularly for the privilege and satisfaction of being a pastoral family team. Over the years, we have found that the rewards and joys far outweigh the challenges and problems. We have tested His promises and they are sure!

Jonas and Raquel and their children are an amazing pastoral leadership family. They truly have wonderful spiritual gifts, a long positive experience, and are one in love, ministry, and service. They have done an excellent job in this book to give very practical counsel and helpful tools for being a team in ministry, thriving as a pastoral family, and how turning challenges and difficult circumstances into opportunities for a blessed ministry. All of this is mixed with a good dose of reality, hope, and encouragement.

Practical helps can be invaluable, but the Arrais family also clearly understands that without Jesus and the daily fresh baptism of the Holy Spirit, we can do nothing of lasting value. But with Him and His Word abiding in us, we can ask anything in His name and He will do it, so we can bear fruit, glorify our Father, and our joy will be full (John 15:5, 7, 8, 11)! This takes quality time with Jesus every day and not just rushing through His presence into our busy activities (*Education,* pp. 260, 261).

Read this book and you will be blessed. But remember that implementing all these wise counsels takes more than human strength. "Not by might, nor by power, but by My Spirit" (Zech. 4:6). "As activity increases and men become successful in doing any work for God there is a danger of trusting to human plans and methods.... Only the work accomplished with much prayer, and sanctified by the merit of Christ, will in the end prove to have been efficient for good" (*The Desire of Ages,* p. 362). Enjoy the fruit and rewards of His Spirit leading your family together in ministry!

Jerry and Janet Page, General Conference Ministerial Secretary, and Associate Ministerial Secretary for Pastoral Families and Prayer Ministries

INTRODUCTION

A growing concern exists around the world today to address the personal needs of pastors and their families. The cry for encouragement, recognition, and support is felt everywhere. In our 35 years of ministry, we have experienced these challenges. While busy serving the church, we have at times forgotten our calling as spouses and parents. We know that responsibilities at home can often be neglected and forgotten, and there are times we get discouraged and frustrated in the ministerial journey. As a result, pastoral and family relationships suffer, marriages struggle, and children grow up resenting the church.

Joys and Challenges of the Pastoral Family offers practical advice on how to face pastoral challenges together as a team ministry. We believe the One who called us for this ministry and life will sustain and strengthen us and our family. This book provides useful instructions on raising children within the dynamics of a pastoral family. It highlights the joy of serving together and the wonderful opportunities ministry provides to the entire family. It also presents insights on how local church leaders can support the pastoral family. We do recognize the different seasons pastors face in their journey, and we offer some practical counsel on each one to help make ministry a joyful experience.

For years we had the desire to share our experience as a pastoral couple. Finally we have this opportunity to help our dear pastoral families around the world. We are familiar with your needs, frustrations, challenges, and dreams. In many ways, we share your experience. The purpose of this book is not to cover everything about the joys of pastoral ministry or to bring a magic solution to the challenges you face, but to give you a glimpse of and a nudge on how to deal with the issues.

The pastoral family today is affected by the complicated burdens and expectations that ministry brings to their lives. But it doesn't have to be this way. We know there is hope for all struggling pastors and their families. We know because we have experienced the agony and the thrill of being a pastoral family. There is hope. This book is about that hope!

Enjoy the reading, and may God bless you!

Jonas and Raquel Arrais

CONTENTS

Acknowledgments

Foreword

Introduction

CHAPTER 1

TEAMING UP IN MINISTRY

"You can do what I cannot do. I can do what you cannot do. Together we can do great things."[1]

Marriage is a sacred union established by God. In it, two individual-ly unique persons become one for the ultimate, sublime purpose of reflecting God's love, justice, mercy, and benevolence to the world. The honor of such a mission, when embraced and fulfilled, results in the success and happiness of the couple. As such, marriage is designed by God to be a win-win-win situation—God wins, the husband wins, and the wife wins. The blessed couple teams up to make decisions together, do things together, share their concerns, and give and receive counsel and suggestions to each other. Each rests in the assurance that their spouse loves them and takes their side when facing the stresses and difficulties of life.

Sharing and reflecting God must be paramount when dealing with the concerns of each spouse, even more so if one is a minister of the gospel. Therefore, the two as a team in ministry are better and stronger when they are a united front in the concerns of God. "They become one flesh" (Gen. 2:24) in spirit, purpose, and mission.

This team dynamic is beneficial and crucial in both marriage and min-istry. Priscilla and Aquila (Acts 18:2, 18, 26) were blessed by upholding this principle. They lived, ministered, taught, hosted, suffered, and succeeded as a team for Christ. Our Lord Himself established this rule with His disciples when He "began to send them out two by two" (Mark 6:7; also see Matt. 10:2–5 and Luke 10:1).

> Calling the twelve about Him, Jesus bade them go out two and two through the towns and villages. None were sent forth alone, but brother was associated with brother, friend with friend. Thus they could help and encourage each other, counseling and praying

together, each one's strength supplementing the other's weakness. In the same manner He afterward sent forth the seventy. It was the Saviour's purpose that the messengers of the gospel should be associated in this way. In our own time evangelistic work would be far more successful if this example were more closely followed.[2]

If the principle of team ministry established by Jesus is applied to the oneness in marriage, great things can be accomplished in the Christian home, mission, pastoral ministry, evangelism, and witnessing. A husband and wife who are committed in mission as in marriage, will complement each other with their individual talents and strengths, and will become a blessing in their home, in the church they serve, and in their community. Even if only one of them is officially recognized as a pastor, God still called both of them. And because they love the Lord, they will love laboring as a team for Him. "The Lord would have ministers and their wives closely united in this work," says Ellen G. White. "The husband and wife can so blend in labor that the wife shall be the complement of the husband."[3]

PARTNERING MINISTRY

No profession in the world requires the involvement of a spouse more than that of being a pastor. The degree of involvement may vary depending on situations, cultures, people, or churches, but, nonetheless, the pastor's spouse is viewed as a partner in the pastor's ministry to the church. The title "pastor's wife" or "pastor's husband" in the case where the wife is the pastor—suggests certain expectations. Learning how to handle them by ignoring the unnecessary, recognizing priorities, and placing the rest in the right perspective, will enhance the spouse's life and contributions in their team ministry.

If you are married to a pastor, consider how God might be glorified through a shared ministry. If you are a pastor, discover ways to create an appropriate environment to involve your spouse in your ministry. What would happen if the two of you were to step outside of your comfort zone and lead a program or event together in your church? A mission trip? A small group study? A pastoral visitation? A shared Sabbath School class? The possibilities are endless! The pastor should show gratitude and appreciation for the spousal involvement and encouragement in their mission. Together, their team ministry becomes strong, efficient, and rewarding.

This partnership will also make the marriage stronger, thereby invigorating the varied approaches to ministry. The way such partnership manifests itself will differ from couple to couple, including those where the pastor is a woman and her husband the supporting spouse.

In sharing the knowledge we have acquired as a ministerial couple, at times each of us, Jonas and Raquel, will present our experience from our unique, individual perspective.

Jonas: At the beginning of my ministry, I didn't know of the concept of having a partnering ministry. Nobody told me how essential it was to build a team ministry with my wife. As a result, many times I neglected her, placing ministry priorities before her. And worst of all, I relegated her to a secondary role. But things have changed. I now understand that without her support I cannot do much. We need each other as we work together, side by side.

The function of Raquel as my helpmate is vital to the success of both our marriage and the church we pastor. And that challenge is reciprocal. We are each other's helpmate to serve each other and God's people. We each seek God's wisdom to do our part faithfully to His pleasure in every aspect of our lives, and we find our challenging roles most fulfilling. Yet, each of us are unique individuals. Hence, every marriage, family, and team ministry is unique in itself. For this reason, no one is more vital to the success of pastors than their spouse. So, pastors need to ask themselves: Am I honoring, acknowledging, and treating my partner in ministry fairly and with dignity?

"The Lord desires them unitedly to watch for His voice, to draw closer and still closer unto Him, feeding upon His Word, and receiving light and blessing to impart to others."[4]

A BIBLICAL PERSPECTIVE

To fully understand the dynamics of team ministry, we need to take a closer look at the biblical origin of marriage and the responsibility Scripture places upon the marriage relationship as it affects couples as husbands and wives, fathers and mothers. The foremost image of marriage in Genesis is the ideal of oneness (Gen. 2:23, 24). Paul uses this image to emphasize the continuity of that oneness in Christian marriage: "For this reason a man will leave his father and mother and be united to his wife, and the two will become one flesh" (Eph. 5:31).

The Christian marriage is not the result of human anthropology or sociology. It is a divine act of creation in which the Creator brought two persons together and made them one. And within the framework of this unity, marriage bears its varied fruits: the ideal relationship of oneness between the two; the thrill of having and rearing children; the sharing of joys and challenges in the journey of life; and journing together to achieve life's goals and purposes, particularly in the pastoral calling where God has placed them as teammates to accomplish His good will. That is what is meant when we say that God designed marriage as a partnership—one that includes all of life's surprises and adventures, and embraces the sacred ministry of serving our Creator and Redeemer.

The concept of oneness between husband and wife becomes palpable to them when they share responsibilities in all areas of their lives: physical, emotional, social, spiritual, and intellectual. Such a sharing involves a purposeful presence in each other's lives. It is this presence that constitutes the unique bond that weaves a husband and wife into one. The couple will discover that next to one's salvation, a marriage lived according to God's design is the most wonderful and satisfying gift one can receive.

THE MESSAGE OF GENESIS 2:18

Consider Genesis 2:18: "The Lord God said, 'It is not good for the man to be alone. I will make a helper [*ezer*] suitable for him.'" Some interpret the word *helper* to mean that the first woman, and all women after her, were designed by God to be man's subordinate and should cater to all of his needs, demands, and whims. Not so. The Hebrew word *ezer* (pronounced "ay-ser"), often translated as helper, is widely misinterpreted to disdain women. It is also used more than a dozen times in the Old Testament to declare that God is our help—yet God is not our subordinate or inferior. The word *ezer* also describes aspects of God's character, none of which are subordinate to any of His other characteristics. That would make no sense. There is no conflict of interest in God's mind. God created mankind in His image, according to His likeness, as male and female (Gen. 1:26, 27). In the account of mankind's creation, God speaks within the unity of a Triune God, for He spoke, "Let Us make . . . in Our image. . . ." And because there is no hierarchy or a cast system in the Divine Family, the human family was created accordingly: in His likeness, as equals. Eve was a helper suitable for Adam in that she was his perfect match, so that together they could be two equal pillars of spiritual strength in their joint commission to represent the character of God in the world.

The woman was created to be a *helpmate* for her husband, that is, a *unique* helper. For example, consider a man trying to carry a sofa. He lifts one end and realizes he needs someone to lift the other end. The person cannot be just any helper. What if a six-year old boy or someone with a broken leg volunteers to help him? That will not work. It must be someone capable and strong enough: a helpmate. An equal! Likewise, the weight of responsibilities of the home must rest upon the shoulders of a man and a woman—when they are bound by love and bring their best to the table, they complement each other. They serve each other. They are equal spiritual columns of support. God provided for the lonesome man in Eden a helpmate for him, thus facilitating with the presence of both a man and a woman, all the blessings God intended to bestow upon the family unit.

A HELPMATE

Raquel: Eve was created to be Adam's helpmate (Gen. 2:18). This is one of the defining purposes of creating woman. I see this purpose as a high calling and unique task. Understanding this is essential for an effective ministry. While it requires a firm commitment and authentic dedication, it will certainly pay off as we see blessings result from it.

As a pastor's spouse, I make sure my husband and I stand together as one. The congregation must not see my husband struggling to minister to them in the role of a lonesome shepherd like Adam once was. No, I make sure they see both of us serving the congregation, for God made me my husband's helpmate for life and for mission. It takes all of me to successfully join my husband in leading the flock in our church. But God is my strength. So I gladly help in many areas of ministry. Some of this help is done at home where no members see. I can intercede in prayer presenting my teammate before God. I can be his source of encouragement. I can be his listening ear. I can share in our burdens and joys. Along with him, I can minister to, instruct, and preserve the immediate circle of our parish, that is, our children. Thus, we embrace our children in our ministry, encouraging them to be springs of joy not only in our home, but also in our congregation and community. In ministry the whole family is in the spotlight, and we have a crucial responsibility to turn on that spotlight to God's glory. Humility, discretion, and clear self-identity are attributes I strive to have. With God's help, I want to be a good pastor's wife, and nothing less. Therefore, I daily surrender my life to my Maker so He can mold me into a vessel that He can use to bless my husband in our home and ministry.

TWO ARE BETTER THAN ONE

Jonas: For more than 30 years, Raquel and I have walked together as a team in pastoral ministry. In this journey, we have had our ups and downs, but it certainly has been a learning and growing experience for both of us. Ecclesiastes 4:9–12 expresses a message that we always read for motivation:

> Two are better than one,
>> because they have a good return for their labor:

If either of them falls down,
  one can help the other up.
But pity anyone who falls
  and has no one to help them up.
Also, if two lie down together, they will keep warm.
  But how can one keep warm alone?
Though one may be overpowered,
  two can defend themselves.
A cord of three strands is not quickly broken.

I stand with God on this one. Holding a thousand dollars in my hand would be awesome, but having two thousand dollars would be twice as awesome! I feel that my wife is the ideal double treasure God has given to me, for she complements my life and makes my ministry more complete. I like what White says: "Through her unselfish interest to advance the cause of God, the wife has made her husband's work much more complete."[5]

Furthermore, "A cord of three strands is not quickly broken" (Eccl. 4:12). When the pastor and spouse make Jesus central in their lives and ministry, they form a three-strand cord, a victorious trio! Jesus must be part of the equation if any venture we undertake is to succeed, more so if our mission is to spread the gospel. Pastor, spouse, and Jesus translate into a powerful partnership, strong enough to care, love, and serve.

Raquel: My husband is more valuable with me than he is without me. And I am more valuable with Jonas than I am without him. We complete each other. I wholeheartedly agree with the above quote from Ecclesiastes. Jonas often says that most pastors would not have made it through seminary school without a loving, unselfish, determined, capable wife who worked full-time, organized their lives, put food on the table, did the laundry, and cared for the children! I have lived that picture. I thank God for His leading when He had me help my husband succeed during his years in the seminary.

AN ESSENTIAL PART IN MINISTRY

Jonas: Dear pastors, your wife is in your corner! She will always vote in your favor. She believes in you when others do not. She lifts you up when others try to tear you down. She calls you up when others call you out! She holds you close when the congregation misunderstands and pushes you away. She fills you up when you are empty. And she makes you laugh when you are at your wit's end. Though you may at times fill overwhelmed, your spouse, standing by you, can help you withstand the ordeal.

That is what Raquel is to me. She is my support. Without her, my pastoral work would have experienced severe limitations. Her support gives me strength, and her standing by me in my ministerial journey has been my inspiration. This support did not come in the form of any official positions she held or activities she performed, but through her affirmation and unconditional commitment to our partnership: the two shall be one. In that oneness, Raquel stands by me through thick and thin, so that my pastoral work is not a one-man struggle, but a team effort. We each feel and fulfill the needs of the other and are both a guide and guardian to each other in our challenging journey.

However, when spousal support is lacking, the consequences are likely to be felt—at times dramatically—because a fruitful pastoral ministry is a plural endeavor when the pastor is married. That is why pastors must keep in mind one important aspect of spousal support in their ministry. Precise statistics are not available, but we have come to the conclusion that, most likely, many Adventist pastors' spouses around the globe work outside of the home and church. If the spouse is employed in a secular setting, and/or if the couple has small children, the supporting spouse can dedicate only a limited amount of time to church activities.

In the case where the wife is the supporting spouse and works outside of the home, she actually holds three jobs: homemaker, employee in another setting, and team ministry partner. She most likely works longer hours than her husband and is under more stress than he is. It would be unfair of him to expect her to be involved in team ministry, if he is unwilling to cooperate in the responsibilities of running their household. This concept at first may be shocking in some cultures, but it should be introduced, by all means. We have already welcomed a woman's financial contribution for the benefit of her family. So let us also welcome and encourage a man's involvement in homemaking, also for the benefit of his family.

A SENSE OF CALLING

Raquel: When you know your calling, you know your ministry. Through the years I have learned (and continue to learn!) to take the good and the bad, criticism and praise, failure and success. Although I know that every woman's experience is different, I believe that if I am a pastor's wife, then God has called me for a reason. The only thing I have to do is to embrace my calling and let God guide me according to His will.

As partners, Jonas and I work effectively in the ministry to which God has called us. We each understand our individual role and serve according to the gifts God has given to each. Working together, we rejoice in experiencing the blessings of seeing our ministry reach new heights as God works through us individually and as a team. In the process, we become instruments of blessing and service to the flock and the community. Such a ministry can be ours only if we have a sense of calling. That calling is threefold:

1. Called by God. My experience as a lifelong partner of my husband, both in family life and in ministry, tells me that my foremost calling is about relationships. These relationships have different dimensions, but all are interlocked. All have the same objective of building God's family—both my family nucleus and my faith family. My calling demands that my primary relationship is with God. It is fundamental to all others: my relationship with myself, my faith journey, and my choices; my relationship with the mate God has given me and the children we have together; and my relationship with the community of believers with whom I worship, witness, serve, and share my faith.

Sometimes pastors' spouses get discouraged and struggle in their role. But one thing all of us can do is to see ourselves as vessels chosen for such a time as this, for such a task as this, and to trust God who has given us the privilege and honor to serve. This is a real joy!

As a pastor's spouse, I pray that you will follow the example of the Lord and walk in love, esteeming each other and delighting in one another. I encourage you to stop trying to live up to everybody else's expectations, trying to please everyone. God wants us to be genuine and He wants to empower us. His love and enduring promises will be our strength and contentment as we keep our hearts open to His guidance.

2. Called to care for my husband. I have also been called to be in a relationship with Jonas. When we exchanged our marital vows, I committed myself to him for life, to be his own, to love him, cherish him, and be part of him in his life, service, joys, and sorrows. I have gladly dedicated my love and life to care for and support my husband. I do not do it because that is what is expected of me; I do it because that is who I am. The biblical directive that in marriage the "two shall be one" lets me know I am needed in both my husband's life and his ministry. When I am involved in church activities, it is important for me to create an atmosphere of love, peace, and contentment for my husband. By doing so, I become an authentic helpmate to him—not just to minister to his needs, but to also assist and protect him. Within this sacred commitment, I become a consoler, good company, an encourager, counselor, good listener, and sympathetic friend to my husband, thereby helping him fulfill his calling as a pastor, and our calling as a ministerial team.

A strong sense of calling is crucial as we embrace ministry. Without it, we will be overwhelmed with the stresses and strains of pastoral life. Why?

Because we are not totally in it. We could easily resent the time and energy that pastoral ministry demands. "God has assigned woman [and even more so, the pastor's wife] her mission; and if she, in her humble way, yet to the best of her ability, makes a heaven of her home, faithfully and lovingly performing her duties to her husband and children, continually seeking to let a holy light shine from her useful, pure, and virtuous life to brighten all around her, she is doing the work left her of the Master."[6]

3. Called to care for my family. Having entered the sacred state of matrimony, I not only have the responsibility to make God the foundation of our relationship and to be committed to my spouse unreservedly, but I also have a binding commitment to the family that followed—to our children who complete our family. We, as a pastoral couple, have pledged to love each other and are committed to making our home a place where our children will grow with the full awareness that our home is a place where God reigns supreme. His love encircles us and our children alike to form a binding unit, and His presence provides an atmosphere where our children can experience what it's like to have a true walk with God. We try to constantly manifest that walk. To that challenging task I have been called, and with heart in hand I answer, "Here I am Lord."

But that is not all. The concept of family goes beyond our home nucleus to embrace our extended family—parents, siblings, in-laws, aunts and uncles, nieces and nephews, and other relatives. As a pastor's spouse, I feel a calling to show our love, care, and concern to all of them, and by so doing, I, along with my husband, demonstrate how Adventist ministry is an inclusive commitment—showing love where love is needed, care where there is neglect, and friendship where there is loneliness.

What we have discussed so far defines a triad of my calling as a pastor's wife, allocating the object of such a call in God, spouse, and family. In addition to that, there are at least four dimensions to the idea of a calling, as pointed out by Rachel Lovingood and Jennifer Landrith[7] and which I have paraphrased here.

- *Specific calling.* This applies to couples who experience a clear-cut call to have their own ministry. They believe God has called them both to become pastor and pastoral spouse. A sense of this specific calling prepares them for the responsibilities that the roles demand. They are ready to go, involved together in team ministry.
- *General calling.* This applies to women and men who believe God has called them to ministry but do not know in what specific area. Like the specific call, they are confident in themselves and how they

are to minister. They have prepared themselves for ministry but not necessarily as a pastor or the spouse of a pastor. Yet they are open to whatever area God calls them.

- *Unexpected calling.* Here we have a couple in non-ministerial professions, but the time comes when one of them (or both) feels called to the ministry. Because of the change in career, they sometimes are not sure about their place in ministry and may feel inadequate. Some of them may not be prepared for this role but they both step into it by faith, believing that if God has called one of them to ministry, then He has also called both of them.

- *Impersonal calling.* This involves men and women who do not feel called to ministry. They view the pastorate as their spouse's job and not their own, and this can cause problems not only in ministry but also in their marriage. Such wives or husbands have no desire to play a supporting role in ministry alongside their spouses, and very often resist becoming involved. They may support the ministry, but only at arm's length, and may regret the fact that their spouse is a pastor.

No matter which of these four dimensions pastors and their spouses fall into, the readiness of both husband and wife to minister is important as they begin laboring in the work God has entrusted to them. Both pastor and spouse should receive "a joint sense of call,"[8] and both should be in total agreement. Without such a call and agreement, a married couple entering in the life of ministry is embarking on a disastrous journey for both their marriage and the church that they serve. When deciding on the course of ministry, Blake Neff says "the couple should proceed as a team and develop or recognize the call together."[9] Without first analyzing and planning to labor as partners in a team ministry, when strain and conflicts surface, it will be difficult for the pastor to serve the church effectively. Consequently, there will be tension at home, which will spill over to their ministry.

UNIQUE CALLING

I grew up as a pastor's kid (PK), and from a very young age I had the desire to work in the ministry of the church. I didn't know if I wanted to marry a pastor and raise my family immersed in ministry. But I did know that God had gifted me in certain areas and designed specific passions that tugged at my heart to serve Him in ministry. The possibility of ministering alongside my husband was a later discovery that God, in His own time, revealed to me and on that I followed.

Whether you have felt a similar call in your life or whether you just happened to fall in love with and married someone who wanted to be in ministry, God has placed you in a unique situation for a distinct purpose. When things are tough, we often find ourselves questioning God's purposes and plans for our lives, our spouse's life, and our ministry. I find much comfort and encouragement in God's promises to fulfill His calling in me as I chose to serve alongside my husband in ministry. One such promise is found in Psalm 139:

> You know when I sit and when I rise;
> you perceive my thoughts from afar.
> You discern my going out and my lying down;
> you are familiar with all my ways. (vv. 2, 3)
> . . . all the days ordained for me were written in your book
> before one of them came to be. (v. 16)

It does not matter whether you felt this call of God from an early age or not. God knew you would be the helpmate your spouse needs. Before you were born, He knew that your days were ordained to be sacrificed, shared, opened, acknowledged, molded, broken, lifted, sifted, and blessed for His ministry. You might dread living in the confines of a pastoral family. You might cringe at being referred to by your spouse position and not your own. You may feel the depth of loneliness at having a lack of close friends within your congregation. You might feel the pain of hearing trusted people tear apart what your spouse is trying so hard to accomplish. You might feel the burden of raising your children under the critical eyes of so many onlookers. The intensity of those emotions is very real. The depth of those struggles can be overwhelming. But when you trust God and allow Him to work in and through you, He will turn those very humbling situations into a blessing for you.

UNIQUE BLESSING

For many pastors' spouses the blessings of their position seem to be few and far between. However, I believe that for all the sacrifices we make for our families, the church, the community, and foremost our heavenly Father, He will bless us again and again. We may not see it at first, we may have to look really hard for it, but those blessings will come. They will be there in many little ways.

One of the greatest blessings I have found in ministry has been the privilege of seeing God at work firsthand. I have had the privilege of witnessing the hand of God moving in peoples' lives and hearts in ways that most people do not get to see.

Being a witness to the miracles performed by God encourages me to be steadfast in prayer. Every time my husband goes out the door to minister, I pray for him and for those involved. Whether I am praying for protection, wisdom, discernment, truth, or just for my husband's safe return, I petition my heavenly Father for my husband to accomplish His work successfully. Being able to petition the Holy Spirit to bless Jonas makes me feel divinely favored.

These blessings are also real for my family. Although others in ministry may not weave their family life into the life of their church, my husband and I have chosen to do so. Our children get to know people they might not otherwise know: good, godly, and wise believers who relate and interact and witness to the truth in their young lives. The children are witnesses to both the good and the bad, and learn that life is a battle between the strong and the frail, between the brave and the timid. God loves each and every person alike, and when we serve others we are ultimately serving Him.

So many women in the world, yet there are so few precious ministry spouses . . . to think that God chose to call me. What a privilege and honor it is to be a pastor's spouse! God has loved, empowered, gifted, and supported us through His Holy Spirit. And when we truly do our service unto the Lord, the blessings in return are indescribable and incomprehensible, the evidence of a gracious and generous God.

QUESTIONS FOR REFLECTION OR DISCUSSION

1. What important insights does Ellen G. White present in the following quotations?

   "The Lord would have ministers and their wives closely united in this work. The husband and wife can so blend in labor that the wife shall be the complement of the husband."[10]

   "When it is possible, let the minister and his wife go forth together. The wife can often labor by the side of her husband, accomplishing a noble work. She can visit the homes of the people and help the women in these families in a way that her husband cannot."[11]

2. Define team ministry.

3. How do cultural influence and traditions affect the understanding of Genesis 2:18?

4. Why is the sense of calling so important in your ministry as a pastor's spouse?

5. How do you describe your unique calling as a helpmate?

ENDNOTES

[1] This quote is often attributed to Mother Teresa, but there is no verification (see http://www.motherteresa.org/08_info/Quotesf.html). Nevertheless, the words are inspiring and relevant to team ministry.

[2] Ellen G. White, *The Desire of Ages* (Mountain View, CA: Pacific Press, 1940), 350.

[3] White, *Manuscript Releases*, 6:43; cf. White, *Pastoral Ministry* (Boise, ID: Pacific Press, 1995), 76.

[4] *Ibid.*

[5] *Ibid.*

[6] White, *Testimonies for the Church* (Mountain View, CA: Pacific Press, 1948), 2:465.

[7] Rachel Lovingood and Jennifer Landrith, *In Our Shoes: Real Life Issues for Ministers' Wives by Ministers' Wives* (Nashville, TN: Lifeway, 2008), 13.

[8] Blake J. Neff, *A Pastor's Guide to Interpersonal Communication: The Other Six Days* (New York: Routledge, 2006), 211.

[9] *Ibid.*

[10] White, *Manuscript Release*, 6:43.

[11] White, *Evangelism* (Washington, DC: Review and Herald, 1946), 491.

CHAPTER 2

CAN WE WORK TOGETHER?

"Coming together is a beginning; keeping together is progress;
working together is success."—Edward Everett Hale

Why should we be partners? One of the great joys in ministry is to see the powerful multiplying effect of synergy—working in partnership with others. We believe that God is always at work around the world, moving His people toward community and collaboration.

For this reason, we believe that serving as a couple has benefits that go beyond bonding, contentment, and peace. There's a sweet intimacy that comes from working together in ministry. Couples who embrace God's call to serve others experience an added closeness, and there are special moments and memories that naturally come when you do things together.

Moreover, participating together in ministry opportunities—whether in your church, neighborhood, community or the world—can also help you grow in your faith as a couple. Working side by side to fulfill the Great Commission—in whatever capacity—deepens your spiritual intimacy like little else can. Being the Lord's witnesses by serving, giving, encouraging, caring, and loving as Jesus loves is rewarding beyond words.

Jonas: It is good to say again, "Two are better than one." Raquel and I share our hearts with each other, and we are amazed at how God has been faithful to us in our journey. We have grown up together. I met her when she was only 15, and we got married three years later when she was 18 and I was 22. Since then we have experienced everything in life together. And we can affirm that partnership works.

Some couples believe and live as if marriage and ministry are at odds with each other because irresolvable conflicts are ever present. They feel that if they both are involved in ministry, in the very process and demands of ministry, there will be a severe neglect of the family. This notion is unfounded.

It arises from the false premise that service to God happens outside of the home and is unrelated to their intimate life.

Other couples believe that marriage and ministry ought to always be in one accord, so they force it to be so by often tweaking and adjusting their lives. Although this does not make home and church effectively harmonize, still they may enjoy some degree of success from their stressful juggling efforts.

Any neglect of a home, including the pastoral home, is clearly against the standards set by God for those who minister in the church. Did Paul not say that the one who oversees the church "must manage his own family well" (1 Tim. 3:4)? Obviously, a pastor cannot manage his home if he is absent most of the time. The crucial point is one of balance between church and home. When the two areas make major and unreasonable demands on the one's time, the pastor, through prayer and careful study, should balance the competing demands without sacrificing the personal need for rest, prayer, and quality time with the spouse. On the other hand, if a pastor wishes to handle all of the demands that come from home and work alone, without sifting the essential from the peripheral, and consumes the proverbial midnight lamp, such a pastor becomes a prime candidate for burnout. Pay attention to this dynamic that impacts the lives of many pastors today.

But there is a better way. This option is to regard marriage and ministry as two sides of the same coin. On the one side are ministry responsibilities such as Bible studies, church administration, singing in the choir, preaching, teaching, counseling, and visitation. On the other side are responsibilities at home, to the spouse, children, and family stewardship. Caring for one side of the coin without neglecting the other—and seeking God's guidance to accomplish both—is the better way of being partners to fulfill God's calling.

There is also a trap that many ministry couples fall into: separating spiritual things from secular matters. God makes no such distinction in our lives. We are to honor and give glory to Him in everything we do in both religious and a secular settings.

PARTNERSHIP BENEFITS

As pastors and their spouses work together, they get a better understanding of the obligations and time required by the ministry, enabling them to better plan in the sharing of responsibilities within the family, including the care and guidance of their children. When they wholeheartedly accepts what God has in store for them individually and as a family, they each will fulfill their assigned role, while jointly living and ministering for God's glory and for family unity.

So, in team ministry, we gain insight and wisdom from each other because our personalities, experiences, and perspectives are individually unique. And we each offer our best for the benefit of the church:

Spiritual growth. A couple that prays and works together as a ministerial team has more potential to grow together spiritually, both as individuals and as a couple. The church's demands and the family's expectations both are on the heart of the pastor. Both roles depend upon God's strength and can be fulfilled rightly only by leaning on Him at all times. As it was promised long ago, "the eternal God is your refuge, and underneath are the everlasting arms" (Deut. 33:27). A pastor's family stands or falls depending on how it stands in its relationship to God. It is not just the pastor who needs this strength. The spouse also needs refuge, strength, and guidance that only God can provide. The couple needs to pray and study the Word together, seeking God's will as a team. By means of and throughout this togetherness process, they will discover the presence of God and the certainty of His guiding strength.

Take, for example, the importance of forgiveness. Often this subject becomes vital within church fellowship. Should the pastor and spouse be drawn into a situation to bring about forgiveness and reconciliation, they would be better equipped to minister if they were good at forgiving in their own relationship.

Prayer strengthens the couple as they individually and jointly place their marriage, family, and the church at the prayer altar every day. Prayer ensures peace, joy, and the strength to meet the demands of daily life in ministry. The prayer life of the couple strengthens and empowers the couple, making their ministry more effective and God-directed.

Strong friendship. Pastoral couples find that, as they minister together, they become closer to each other not only as a couple but as friends. Many pastoral couples express that their spouse is their best friend. Best friends try to be together and share their lives as much as possible. The pastor and spouse who are ministry partners and best friends understand this fact and the reality that their spouse is the only person who can and will be their helpmate.

A husband and wife who work appropriately together in marriage and ministry grow closer as a team, and the relationship they build will become stronger and last a lifetime. And the church will be blessed by seeing the couple laughing, joking, or even crying together as they share their victories and failures. Such a close bond creates a positive witness to a strong marriage. "The family tie is the closest, the most tender and sacred, of any on earth. It was designed to be a blessing to mankind. And it is a blessing wherever the marriage covenant is entered into intelligently, in the fear of God, and with due consideration for its responsibilities."[1]

We were great friends before our wedding, but we are better friends now. We see God using our meager talents to move people forward in their lives, to help them experience the richness of life and the swiftness of the spiritual race.

Church benefits. As a couple works together, they become a blessing to the church. The partnership benefits not only their spiritual life, but their everyday life as well. The church sees in a dynamic pastoral team a model for true Christian family values and a model for the ministry of the church by which both the pastoral couple and the church members can join hands to advance God's cause in the community where they live. By serving together in one united ministry, the couple must model for other couples how to make their own lives more effective as witnesses for God's kingdom. Thus, the path to serving God and His people in the church will become clear and fruit-bearing.

Another benefit the church experiences from a team ministry in which husband and wife are partners is the shared gender-based ministry the pastor and spouse can have. Each of them can serve as a mentor for men and women of the church respectively. Where both team members are so engaged, they establish strong ministries for women and men, addressing the needs of each group, and fostering the spiritual growth of both together in home and church contexts.

PARTNERSHIP'S BEST PRACTICES

Partnership awards the ability to accomplish more together. It confirms that a team is stronger than a single person laboring alone. We need each other. It has been said that, it is better to have one person working with you than three working for you. Here are eight partnership practices that will strengthen and sustain an effective husband-and-wife ministry team:[2]

1. Allow God to define your combined ministry. A pastor-spouse team should have an idea of what expectations each is to meet and what roles each is to fill. But God does the calling and equipping. Be open to encouragement and critique from others, but remember to whom you both must ultimately answer.

2. Take time to communicate. The first step towards making a marriage affair-proof is to determine that both of you are committed to your marriage, and that you will do everything possible to let that relationship remain strong. Every marriage can be a better marriage. Turn off the electronic devices, put down that absorbing book, and just talk and listen to each other. Time spent in mutual communication is quality time and never a waste.

3. *Avoid bringing church problems home.* Remember that you and your spouse are on the same page. When issues and frustrations at church arise, do not take your frustrations out on your spouse. Very often you will need to draw boundaries between marriage and ministry. If ministry begins to affect your relationship, stop and re-evaluate what is happening. Repair the breach to prevent a flood.

4. *Resolve disagreements daily.* An unresolved disagreement is a leading factor in relational deterioration. If your spouse is upset with you, listen and ask for forgiveness (even if you are not totally in the wrong). And if you are upset with your spouse, talk about it with them, forgive, and move on. Remember Paul's counsel: "Do not let the sun go down while you are still angry" (Eph. 4:26). Prayerfully work it out. Your ministry and flock depend on it.

5. *Minister spiritually to each other.* Your first ministry responsibility begins at home. Team ministry requires ensuring that you minister to each other first before you go to your flock. Do you pay sufficient attention to enrich your marriage? Do you care for your spouse's needs—physical, emotional, social, intellectual, and spiritual? Do you pray together? Do you study the Bible together? The time and energy you spend with each other will encourage others to also have a fruitful ministry.

6. *Affirm each other.* Use every opportunity to affirm each other. Do not hesitate to say how much you mean to each other. Sharing words of affection, encouragement, thanksgiving and affirmation, doing things as tokens of caring for each other, and remembering important dates (birthdays, anniversaries, etc.) do much in cementing the relationship. You can never over-affirm your spouse's contribution to your happiness and wellbeing by expressing how much you love and appreciate their part in enriching your life and ministry.

7. *Seek to understand each other.* Resolve to help your spouse realize all of their God-given potentials. Find opportunities for them to shine, and take pride in the person with whom God has teamed you up. There is no one like your spouse. You were tailor-made for each other.

8. *Live life together.* When you have time away from ministry, use your moments of leisure to spend quality time together. What activities do you both enjoy? Participate in them together because shared experiences add to your common treasure vault of memories. And for activities that only one spouse enjoys, take turns participating in it. That way, both of you will have an opportunity to live the other's uniqueness. Be amazed at who the person you love is, and your bond of marriage will grow stronger.

REMUNERATION FOR PASTOR'S WIVES

Jonas: I cannot ignore this important issue while talking about teaming up in ministry. In some places, I see a growing concern regarding the remuneration of pastors' spouses who are engaged in some kind of ministry to the church. We need to understand that when a conference or a church hires a pastor, they are not getting two for the price of one. Most pastors' spouses are dedicated and willing to give themselves to the work of the church. However, this should not be taken for granted. If spouses are expected to work in the ministry and for the church, they should be remunerated.

Ellen G. White speaks about this quite extensively. In one place, she writes:

> Injustice has sometimes been done to women who labor just as devotedly as their husbands, and who are recognized by God as being necessary to the work of the ministry. The method of paying men-laborers, and not paying their wives who share their labors with them, is a plan not according to the Lord's order. . . . God is a God of justice, and if the ministers receive a salary for their work, their wives, who devote themselves just as disinterestedly to the work, should be paid in addition to the wages their husbands receive, even though they may not ask for this.[3]

White is not suggesting that a monthly salary be given to pastors' spouses who stay home to take care of the children or participate in church activities as a normal member of the congregation. The counsel is applicable to those spouses who work full-time or part-time for the church, visiting church members, giving Bible studies, and assisting in other pastoral duties.

CONCLUSION

God wants us to succeed. But we must be aware of and heed the apostle Peter's warning that the enemy is lurking (1 Pet. 5:8), and waits patiently for the opportunity to devour and destroy us. As partners in team ministry, we are to be wise, aware, and alert, on the lookout for each other and pressing forward in our ministry without any distraction or deviation. Being sensitive to God's voice and connecting into God's word daily will provide a safe path.

Enjoy your shared ministerial life and make it a success! Remember, the calling of God is irrevocable unless you choose to walk away from it. But if you have made your calling and election sure (2 Pet. 1:10), you will enjoy the ministry for life. Along with your spouse, your team ministry will reflect your strengths and commitment. Standing together, with Christ as your foundation and center of your marriage and mission, you will neither stumble nor be shaken. Team ministry translates into glory for God, strength for your church, and abiding love for both of you.

QUESTIONS FOR REFLECTION OR DISCUSSION

1. What are the benefits of doing ministry with your spouse?
2. How can spouses who work outside the home and church still be involved in teams ministry?
3. Which partnership's best practices need to be included in your life?
4. Why is it important to remunerate a pastor's spouse who is actively involved in ministry?
5. Share your personal experience on how you support your spouse in ministry.

ENDNOTES

1 Ellen G. White, *The Ministry of Healing* (Mountain View, CA: Pacific Press, 1942), 356.

2 Adapted from Larry and Judi Keefauver, "*Put Your Wife in Her Place . . . as a Ministry Partner, That Is,*" *Ministry Today*, February 28, 2005, http://ministrytoday-mag.com/leadership/women-in-leadership/10660, accessed April 21, 2014 Used with permission.

3 White, *Gospel Workers* (Washington, DC: Review and Herald, 1948), 452, 453.

CHAPTER 3

IF YOU WANT TO MARRY A PASTOR

"As God by creation made two of one, so again by marriage He made one of two."—Thomas Adam

Many men and women throughout the world study theology and commit their lives to spreading the gospel. If you want to marry a pastor, this chapter is for you. In our case, Jonas is the pastor and Raquel the spouse. Therefore, we will be addressing this chapter's theme from our perspective.

He is a pastor for all seasons. His smile reflects genuine kindness and warmth. He stands with his cheerful wife and greets worshippers with a welcome that springs from a deep well of care and authentic friendship for his church. When he stands at the pulpit, he radiates a Spirit-filled aura. When he opens the Bible, God's Word leaps out, touching the worshippers with just the message they need. To the discouraged, he points to the Great Shepherd for an embrace of courage and hope. To the youth, his words come as a challenge to walk steady, climb higher, and run the course faithfully. To those who find the Christian walk at times joyful and at times worrisome, he finds the right words and gives the right direction. Under his prayerful leadership and Spirit-filled guidance, the church grows, evangelism marches onward, Christian education nurtures the young, and believers are fed and nurtured. The congregation testifies, "Our pastor is the ideal minister."

Or so you think.

As a single woman on the verge of deciding your career and charting your future, you may think, "It would be nice, God willing, for me to find a man like that; my life would be perfect." So you decide, "I am going to marry a pastor just like him." But before you make a firm decision, we counsel you to pause for a moment.

BEFORE YOU DECIDE

The role of a pastoral spouse is an unenviable one. The life of a pastor's spouse is not one of eternal bliss and perfection that you may imagine. Your pastoral couple may look great on the outside, but between them and within the confines of their home, there are challenges: relational, interpersonal, financial, social, even spiritual. If a pastoral couple were honest and allow you a look into their private lives, you may discover that what looks like a bed of roses from the outside, in fact, is a bed of nails. Allow us to clue you in on what you may find.

A HUMAN BEING

Pastors are human beings like everyone else. God may have called them to the ministry and anointed them to lead His flock, but the pastors are people with needs, emotions, longings, pressures, obligations, temptations, struggles, failures—just like anyone else. Being called to the ministry does not mean that one is called to be a superman, free from the ups and downs of ordinary life. You will see in a minister that strange dichotomy of the anointed man of God on Sabbaths and the all-too-human person the rest of the week. In fact, the pressures of life—in the sacred call to ministry, the call to be a faithful spouse and parent, and the call to be an honorable member of the community—are perhaps more divergent, difficult, and stringent for pastors than for people with other callings in life. Contrary to what may be popular opinion, being a pastor is not all that glamorous or easy. It is a job that demands great sacrifice and offers little reward.

THE MINISTER'S PARAMOUNT CALL

When you marry a pastor, you are marrying a person whose love and commitment for Jesus needs to be paramount in his life and ministry, and so it should be in your life as well. Ellen G. White writes of the importance of letting Christ reign in a marriage:

> Only this can prevent the grievous wrongs which so often embitter married life. Only where Christ reigns can there be deep, true, unselfish love. Then soul will be knit with soul, and the two lives will blend in harmony.[1]

As a pastor's spouse, would you embrace Jesus and His ministry and make the calling by Jesus as much yours as it is your spouse's?

If you marry a pastor, you are marrying someone who has a prior and supreme call on his life. This means that where God calls pastors must go.

They make a commitment to follow Jesus no matter where that may take them—in the inner city, the rural countryside, or even another country. In the middle of the night they may have to visit a parishioner who has been rushed to the hospital and needs his pastor to come and minister to him. Many times it may seem the church has priority over family. It is not so. Pastors are just being obedient to God's call. The pastor is God's first. In that context, your comfortable lifestyle may be stretched beyond your wildest imagination.

Many, when confronted with these challenges of being pastor's spouse, back off. Desiring to marry a pastor is a good thing, but the good comes at a high price—the price of the high calling of ministry that binds both the pastor and the spouse.

SIDE BY SIDE

Marrying a pastor is not the same as marrying a lawyer or doctor. The spouse of a lawyer cannot give legal advice to clients; that is against the law. And the spouse of a doctor is not allowed inside of the operating room during surgery. But in a church community, pastors need spouses to stand by them in ministry. Whether they are officially appointed or not, they should be respected and recognized by the church as the pastor's right hand.

At times, pastoral spouses may see themselves laboring without a defined title or job description, without a clear identity. Yet in gratitude they respond to the calling and wear the many hats the role requires. They understand the priorities of ministry, desire to study and share the Word with others, and have a burden to reach out to the struggling souls within the congregation. They are the godly helpmates that pastors need by their side.

Pastoral work calls for caring, serving, feeding, and guiding the flock God has given. However, if pastoral spouses do not share the same vision and commitment, the work of God may suffer. And going forward, the ministry may become a burden to both of them. White reminds us of the importance of the wife's involvement in ministry:

> With meekness and humility, yet with a noble self-reliance, she should have a leading influence upon minds around her, and should act her part and bear her cross and burden in meeting, and around the family altar, and in conversation at the fireside. The people expect this, and they have a right to expect it. If these expectations are not realized, the husband's influence is more than half destroyed.[2]

Let's be real—if deep down in your heart you do not enjoy pastoral ministry, then you should not marry a pastor. It would not be fair to you or the ministry. It would not be right to give the impression that you are the right person to be a pastoral spouse, when in reality you do not share his same desire and vision. God may have another plan for your life where you may serve Him better.

ARE YOU CALLED TO BE A PASTOR'S SPOUSE?

Before you even decide to date a pastor or a would-be pastor, pray about it and seek God's direction and counsel. We believe that where God guides, He provides; if He calls, He enables. "As the will of man co-operates with the will of God, it becomes omnipotent. Whatever is to be done at His command may be accomplished in His strength. All His biddings are enablings."[3] If being a pastor's wife is God's plan for you, you will face this sacred and immense challenge because it is Christ who strengthens you. The cost is great, but the rewards will be greater. And to help you determine whether or not you should be a pastoral spouse, consider the following:

1. A pastor lives his work. Ministry is one of the most unpredictable jobs one could have. It is not uncommon for a pastor to devote ten to twelve hours every day to ministry-related activities. When on vacation and travelling with family, his work follows him. You will find him preaching or teaching Sabbath School in that remote church he is visiting; he obliges to their invitation because he is committed to his calling. And even on days off at home, a pastor's mind is on his work: sermon preparation, parish needs, and planning church related events.

2. Pastors live for others. Pastoring is about helping, serving, and being surrounded by people. Serving others is the pastor's way to serve God. As Paul, the pastor of pastors, affirms, "Whatever you do, work at it with all your heart, as working for the Lord, not for human masters. . . . It is the Lord Christ you are serving" (Col. 3:23, 24).

3. Pastors face financial constraints. Ministry is a highly blessed profession, although not a highpaying one. The majority of pastors face financial struggles from time to time. While many non-Adventist ministers get huge salaries—televangelists, prosperity preachers, pastors of megachurches—they are the exception to the rule. As an average pastoral spouse, you will not live in a mansion with hired help. In fact, to supplement the pastor's income, you may feel the need to find another job.

In ministry, pastors have many more challenges than just these three. Are you willing to stand through thick and thin with someone who lives his work, lives for others, has financial struggles, and faces many difficulties? By being aware of the reality of these challenges, you are now better informed to make that very serious decision: Should you marry a pastor?

WORDS OF CAUTION

You may have numerous reasons for wanting to marry that young pastor. The man you are attracted to is a godly person, refined, educated, well mannered, social, caring, and helpful. Someone who loves the Lord, is an effective preacher, knows the Bible, communicates well from the pulpit, is spiritually strong, is morally upstanding, and cares for people. And you may have a hundred other reasons why you feel your marriage to that pastor will be just ideal. But look for any caution signals ahead.[4]

1. Do not marry a pastor if you do not have a similar calling from God. Your expectations will be misdirected and unfulfilled, and both of you will be perpetually frustrated if you do not have a calling from God for the sacred task of being a pastor's spouse. You may ask, "Where in the Bible do you find God calling ministers' spouses?" Nowhere. It is just basic common sense. You will not find in the Bible God calling artists or agriculture specialists or communication consultants, but every field of study and career has people gifted in these areas, people who can testify of God's calling of them. So it is in ministry. You may not have special training or a formal calling, but you must have a deep abiding love for the gospel, a respect for and an understanding of ministry, and a willingness to share yourself in the joys and sufferings of being part of a pastor's life. If you do not have such a strong commitment within you, do not marry a pastor. Does not the Bible say, "Can two walk together, unless they are agreed?" (Amos 3:3, NKJV).

2. Do not marry a pastor if you are not a person of prayer. "Prayer is the breath of the soul." "It is the secret of spiritual power. No other means of grace can be substituted, and the health of the soul be preserved. . . . Neglect the exercise of prayer, or engage in prayer spasmodically, now and then, as seems convenient, and you lose your hold on God. The spiritual faculties lose their vitality, the religious experience lacks health and vigor."[5] A spouse rooted deeply in prayer will be a blessing in the life of a pastor, inspiring him to effectively serve God and minister to His people. As Luke 18:1 says, we "should always pray and not give up."

So, do not think about marrying a pastor if you cannot in all sincerity let prayer be your breath and its power be the strength of your life, focused on the following inspired words: "Not that we are competent in ourselves to claim anything for ourselves, but our competence comes from God" (2 Cor. 3:5).

3. Do not marry a pastor if you expect him to be at home most of the time. Ministry is very demanding timewise, and varied in its schedule. A pastor does not work according to within a fixed schedule. Even if the schedule has time allotted for office, visitation, study, and so forth, there are quite often emergencies or unforeseen last-minute calls. As a result, the pastor may come home late or miss an appointment with the spouse or family. Subsequently, tension may develop between a pastor and his family, because both sides of the coin are competing for and demanding the pastor's time. Thus, the unexpected demands from the parish and the expected demands from the family keep ministry ever in a challenging mode. The pastor may feel helpless and in need of understanding. If you cannot provide that help and understanding, walk away from marrying a pastor. A pastor, it is said, must pray for two essentials in his life: wisdom and an understanding spouse.

4. Do not marry a pastor if you are not sensitive to people's need. Ministry is not an isolated occupation. It involves people—the hurting, lonely, sick, needy, grateful, rejoicing, etc. The pastor is expected to speak to their needs and provide for their spiritual growth and nourishment. If you, as a pastor's spouse, cannot be loving and supportive of people, you will find it difficult to appreciate or understand pastoral ministry. But if you are ready to say, "Your people will be my people" (Ruth 1:16), you meet the basic prerequisite to take the challenging journey of being part of a pastoral couple.

5. Do not marry a pastor if you want a private life. A pastor does not live in a vacuum. In his work, he is often expected to listen to church members, listen to their problems, offer counsel, or pray with them.

> People are easily reached through the avenues of the social circle. . . . It is highly important that a pastor should mingle much with his people, that he may become acquainted with the different phases of human nature, readily understand the workings of the mind, adapt his teachings to the intellect of his people, and learn that grand charity possessed only by those who closely study the nature and needs of men.[6]

Thus, a pastor's wife is expected to understand the importance of a pastor relating well with his parishioners. One thing is promised: "From your home, you will see the worst side of the best people (God's children). But determine that you will love them anyway, and God will use you in amazing ways."[7] If you cannot make this determination, or if this issue will be too challenging for you, it will not be wise to marry a pastor.

6. Do not marry a pastor if you expect earthly rewards. If you marry a pastor expecting high rewards in terms of wealth, position, or recognition, you are in for a big disappointment. Ministry is never a call for rewards here on earth, but a call for service—to take up the cross, follow Jesus, and proclaim the good news of the gospel wherever the Lord leads. The payoff for God's servants comes not in earthly recognitions and financial gain, but in the promises of God in His appointed time. If we believe in and trust our lives to God, the blessings of those promises will be awarded spiritually and in other ways throughout our lives as the Lord deems best. And, ultimately, we will be "repaid at the resurrection of the righteous" (Luke 14:14).

7. Do not marry a pastor without first analyzing yourself. You must take a good look at yourself. Has God called you to be a pastor's spouse? Have you considered the cost and sacrifices are involved? Are you ready to walk hand-in-hand, united in spirit with your spouse through the rugged terrain of ministering to God's people? Talk to your Lord. Seek His guidance. If you discover that, for sure, God is leading you to marry a minister, then take that step in prayer and commitment, and trust that God will lead you to the right person for a lifetime of satisfaction in knowing you followed God's guidance and made a lasting difference in people's lives.

"I COULD NEVER BE A PASTOR'S WIFE"

Gabriele Rienas, a pastor's wife and counselor, has an excellent answer to someone who had not planned on being a pastor's spouse. Here is her paraphrased advice[8]:

I am a pastor's wife. When women learn this out about me, they often give me a startled look. Invariably it includes the interjection, "I could never be a pastor's wife." Evidently, they assume that the role is something exhausting and difficult, requiring some great and lofty talents they lack.

The truth is a lot simpler. Most of us came to this role without specifically asking or planning for it. There may be women who intentionally sought out and married a minister because of a strong desire to be a pastor's wife. But in the experience of others, including me, such was not the case. Most of us simply fell in love with someone and pledged our life and future to someone who already had or would receive a call to serve God in ministry.

But I do have good news for you. The roles and responsibilities that go along with being a minister's wife are as diverse and individualistic as you are. Defining yourself as a pastor's wife should be similar to the process of breaking in a fine pair of shoes. You start with an adequate fit at the store, but it doesn't quite fit until you wear them for a while, letting them mold to your feet, eventually feeling like a second skin. You start by being yourself and then, by experience, grow into a place that fits you without any discomfort.

Here are four suggestions to help you overcome any hesitation you may have about becoming a pastor's wife:

1. Free yourself of unrealistic expectations. Do not be something you are not, nor have the desire to ever be. Unfortunately, in some circles people believe that the pastor's wife should carry out her role in a certain fixed way. A pastor's wife should look, act, serve, dress, and so forth in the expected manner. While some rise to the occasion and fill the shoes splendidly, others feel overwhelmed before they even start trying. If the job seems too big or overwhelming, we suggest the problem is with the expectations, not the job itself. We are not suggesting you should not strive to become better. However, your expectations for growth need to match your own situation and calling.

2. Recognize that you do have a calling. It is a calling to serve God with your whole heart, using the particular set of talents He has given you. It is a calling to grow and become more of what God expects you to be. Every believer is called to this task.

You are a unique woman of God, called for a purpose that is also unique. You also are (or are going to be) married to a minister who has a passion and vision to pursue the call that is his. His calling will, to some degree, influence where you live, with whom you interact, and with what you will be involved. Blending your lives together becomes a journey of discovery. It helps a great deal if your husband is on the same page when it comes to his expectations of you. If he is not, this is something you need to address as a couple.

3. Approach challenges together. Pastoring comes along with its own unparalleled challenges. A few of them are time, expectations, and stress. Again, these challenges will certainly affect your home and marriage. You need to approach them together. Speak with your husband about your feelings and concerns. Become each other's ally and solve problems together. A team effort will keep you from feeling alone in your struggle. Seek outside help if this is a problem.

4. Be yourself. Learn what that means. Above all, ask for God's help and know that His favor is yours. His expectation is that you would first and foremost seek Him and grow into His love. Once you feel free to stop striving, the rest comes more easily.

God has done his part, and Christian activity is needed now. God calls for this. He expects his people to bear a part in presenting the light of truth to all nations. Who will enter into this partnership with the Lord

Jesus Christ? He will prescribe the terms, he will make all the conditions. Has God enlightened you with a knowledge of himself? Have the treasures of his word been opened to your understanding, so that you have become intelligent in regard to the truths therein? Then go to work with your ability. If you are only humble, pure in heart, single in purpose, you will see the needs and wants of God's cause.[9]

COUNSEL TO SINGLE PASTORS

Ministry is not like any other profession or business. To preach the gospel of Jesus Christ and be involved in caring for His people is the highest privilege and the loftiest work one can have on this earth. It is a personal calling and can come only from Christ. It demands total devotion and unreserved dedication to the Savior and His blood-bought family. Prayer, Bible study, counsel from experienced ministers, and a sense of calling must precede a decision to prepare for the ministry. "The greatest work, the noblest effort, in which men can engage is to point sinners to the Lamb of God. True ministers are co-laborers with the Lord in the accomplishment of His purposes."[10]

If you choose to be a pastor, you are not going to enter the ministry alone. Most likely, you will have a partner with you. And that partner should be chosen wisely, and with much study and prayer. Marrying the wrong person can make life in any profession difficult, but in ministry, it can be disastrous. John Wesley, an English cleric and theologian, married a woman who did not share his call to ministry. The marriage strained their personal lives and made his ministry difficult. J. Oswald Sanders, a great preacher and writer, said it well: "A man must have a wife who fully shares his spiritual aspirations and is willing to make necessary sacrifices."[11] The spouse should have a clear calling to serve God in this capacity. Wesley's wife did not have this calling, and, therefore, Wesley had a difficult time balancing family and ministry.

And so, a couple that does not share in the call of God could be considered an unequally yoked. The challenges faced in such a situation could be as great as in a marriage between two people who do not have the same spiritual belief system. Ministry is difficult work, but it can be "especially tough if . . . spouses are not supportive"[12] of the same focused ministry. It is imperative, therefore, that a pastor finds in his would-be spouse someone who shares the call to ministry and accepts the challenges and promises of that calling.

If you are a seminarian or already in the ministry, ask yourself the following questions before you make a final decision on who your spouse will be:

1. Feels secure in the relationship. A spirit of insecurity, and sometimes jealousy, can do irreparable damage to both your marriage and ministry. As a pastor, you will have to minister and relate to your parishioners of both genders. You will need to do this in a responsible and open manner, particularly when it comes to ministering to the opposite sex. It is vital that your spouse knows this in order to avoid petty jealousy that can ruin your ministry, family, and life. A minister's spouse should be relatable, because by virtue of association with the minister, the spouse will have to relate with people without being too sensitive and personal.

2. Understands and expects changes in schedule. The work and appointment schedule of a minister is not etched in stone. However well planned, the schedule is subject to disruptions and emergencies. And the pastor must tend to the needs of the congregation during critical moments of their lives. This can throw a pastor's calendar into total disarray to the dismay of his family. Therefore, a spouse that does not understand such emergencies might feel frustrated, hence frustrating the pastor as well. It is good to be organized, but the Lord's work often requires spontaneous reaction and obedience that may go contrary to plans. As a minister, if there is ever a clash between your will and God's will, it is only wise that God's will prevails, because at the end of the day, true ministry is all about God. Does your spouse understand this?

3. Understands the pastoral role can be very demanding. A pastor's spouse who constantly wants her husband by her side is asking too much. Some ministers travel all week and sometimes for months depending on the nature of their assignment. Although the pastor should work out a balanced work schedule and spend sufficient time with his family, a spouse that understands and accepts that a pastor's commitments differ greatly from the schedule of the accountant next door, will be a welcome blessing to the pastor.

4. Understands the pastor's financial limitations. We have already mentioned this, but it merits a second look. A minister has to serve under financial limitations. If the spouse is excessively fond of material things and shopping is a favorite pastime, that could hinder not only their relationship, but also the pastor's ministry.

> When we love God supremely, temporal things will occupy their right place in our affections. If we humbly and earnestly seek for knowledge and ability in order to make a right use of our Lord's goods, we shall receive wisdom from above. When the heart leans to its own preferences and inclinations, when the thought is cherished that money can confer happiness without the favor of God, then the money becomes a tyrant, ruling the man.[13]

CONCLUSION

Finally, as a couple who has spent all of our adult lives in ministry, and are also happily married, let us share with you these concluding thoughts. We are a team called by God, under God, and we support each other in the wonderful adventure of ministry. During these years of ministry and marriage we have discovered that pastors and their ministry will not surpass the quality, effectiveness, and growth of their marital relationship. If their marriage is healthy, their ministry has a much greater probability of being productive and effective. Conversely, if their marriage is wilting, their ministry will be extremely limited and greatly affected. Here is some practical counsel for every ministry couple to consider:

Seek premarital advice. Before getting married, consider seeking counsel on issues discussed in this chapter. Be honest about the weaknesses you see in each other. The heartache of a broken engagement pales in comparison to the agony of an unhappy or failed marriage.

Delight in the Lord. Approach every situation and decision with the question, "What is going to please the Lord?" The psalmist replies: "Delight yourself in the Lord; and He will give you the desires of your heart" (Ps. 37:4). Hence, it is the Lord who gives the gift of a wife or husband. "He who finds a wife finds what is good and receives favor from the Lord" (Prov. 18:22).

Consistency. Pray together daily. The last thing the spouse of the pastor needs to see is a different person at home than the one in the pulpit. This is especially true when children enter into your life. "Consistency is a jewel. Our faith, our dress, and our deportment must be in harmony with the character of our work, the presentation of the most solemn message ever given to the world."[14] Therefore, be consistent in your life and daily walk with Christ. Then your calling to ministry will be a blessing to the church you serve and the wife you love.

Always remember that God has great plans for each of you. Just make sure His plans include marrying each other by seeking His will. Before every big decision, surrender to God and pursue holiness. Trust in the Lord and His promises to make your paths straight (Prov. 3:5, 6). God's plan for your lives is extraordinary! Do you want to discern His will for you? We encourage you to personalize Paul's prayer: "We ask God to fill you with the knowledge of his will, with all the wisdom and understanding that his Spirit gives. Then you will be able to live as the Lord wants and will always do what pleases him" (Col. 1:9, 10, TEV).

QUESTIONS FOR REFLECTION OR DISCUSSION

1. In your opinion, what are the most important things to consider before marrying a pastor?
2. List some of the challenges to consider before marrying a pastor. Explain.
3. In your opinion, why should marrying a pastor be considered a call from God?
4. Why do pastors face more marriage challenges today than previously? What can couples do to reduce or overcome such challenges?
5. Why did you marry a pastor? Share your personal experience.

ENDNOTES

[1] Ellen G. White, *Testimonies for the Church* (Mountain View, CA: Pacific Press, 1948), 5:362.

[2] White, *Gospel Workers* (Washington, DC: Review and Herald, 1915), 201.

[3] White, *Christ's Object Lessons* (Washington, DC: Review and Herald, 1941), 333.

[4] Adapted from Joe McKeever, "Why You May Not Want to Marry a Preacher," Charisma News, October 10, 2015, http://www.charismanews.com/opinion/52510, accessed July 12, 2017. Used with permission.

[5] White, *Gospel Workers*, 254, 255.

[6] White, *Testimonies for the Church*, 4:266.

[7] Joe McKeever, "Why You May Not Want to Marry a Preacher," http://www.charismanews.com/opinion/52510. Accessed July 24, 2017.

[8] Adapted from Gabriele Rienas, "I Never Wanted to Be a Pastor's Wife," *Enrichment Journal*, http://enrichmentjournal.ag.org/201201/201201_114_NeverWanted.cfm, accessed July 12, 2017. Used with permission.

[9] White, "Partakers of the Divine Nature," *The Advent Review and Sabbath Herald*, March 1, 1887.

[10] White, *Gospel Workers*, 18.

[11] J. Oswald Sanders, *Spiritual Leadership* (Chicago, IL: Moody Press, 1980), 57.

[12] Thom S. Rainer, *Seven Things to Consider If Your Spouse Is Not Supportive of Your Ministry*, March 4, 2015, http://thomrainer.com/2015/03/seven-things-consider-spouse-supportive-ministry/, accessed July 7, 2015.

[13] White, *The Adventist Home* (Nashville, TN: Southern Publishing Association, 1952), 372.

[14] White, *Evangelism* (Washington, DC: Review and Herald, 1946), 541.

— CHAPTER 4 —

THE ROLE OF THE PASTORAL SPOUSE

"Encourage one another and build each other up."
—1 Thessalonians 5:11

Being a pastor's spouse comes with an abundance of grace and struggle. Some spouses are gifted by God with leadership abilities, and they have a natural passion to serve in any way. Others have to struggle to fulfill certain roles placed upon them by the congregation. Therefore, it is important that the pastor makes it clear from the beginning that "his wife has unique strengths, weaknesses, interests, and ministry desires," and that "her ministry is determined by God's giftedness to her and her freedom to choose to what degree and in what capacity to use it."[1]

Being a pastor's spouse is not simply a role to be filled—to stand by the pastor and greet the worshippers as they leave the church at the end of the Sabbath service; to welcome a visitor who drops by the house to talk to the pastor; to organize a potluck; or to attend to a phone call from a parishioner. These may be necessary, but a pastor's spouse is called for a spiritual purpose, not just to fulfill such tasks. The spouse of the shepherd of the congregation shares the ministry to bring glory to the Lord as they unitedly worship and serve, and to be a blessing to the congregation to which they minister.

As such, "pastor's wife" is not a title one bears, not an act one performs, but a ministry in which she works serving in the background, yet unmistakably letting the congregation know she is there to share her husband's needs, burdens, cares, concerns, and involvement in fulfilling God's will. As a pastor's wife, she tells her congregation that they can count on her in prayer, fellowship, pain, and consistent growth in God's grace. "A minister's wife should ever have a leading influence on the minds of those with whom she associates, and she will be a help or a great hindrance. She either gathers with Christ or scatters abroad."[2]

The pastor's wife needs to be open-minded and have the right attitude for what God is doing in her life. She may be given the opportunity to minister in ways that she never dreamed about. Similarly, church members must understand that the ministries in which she labors are "God-given callings, not expectation-fulfilling burdens."[3]

A LIFE OF CHALLENGES

The life of a pastor's spouse is one of many challenges and is never easy. She is expected to smile and be cheerful even when she may be distraught about something or have many hurdles to overcome. She must accept criticism gracefully. Her home is often taken over by visitors, and she is expected to cater to them and be ready to entertain. Besides that, she must run her household like clockwork: cooking, cleaning, running errands, etc. And, of course, she is expected to raise model children while remaining cool, calm, and serene through it all. She should dress well—with modesty and good taste. Though the phone rings constantly, she must not show any irritation, answering each time pleasantly and courteously. She is the "unpaid servant" of the church and often expected to fill every job no one else wants. Even if she has young children, she is still expected to fulfill her "duty" to the parish, though others may relinquish theirs for the same reason of having too much on their plate.

Yet a committed pastor's wife is ever by her husband's side, and throughout difficulties she always sides with her husband. Often she is a silent partner—sharing his disappointments and joys, his apparent failures and frequent challenges. She steps quietly into the background as many applaud him. Even in that quietness she finds fulfillment. She is not perfect, but she serves a perfect Lord who is always available for her to lean on.

A LIFE OF ADVENTURES

In the midst of many challenges, the life of a pastor's wife can be full of adventure. She can be her authentic self and trust God to work through her in powerful ways. "The wives of ministers should live devoted, prayerful lives. . . . If they would only lean confidingly, in childlike trust, upon God, and have their affections centered in Jesus, deriving their life from Christ, the living Vine, what an amount of good they might do, what a help they might be to others, what a support to their husbands, and what a reward would be theirs in the end!"[4]

While the rewards at the end of the journey are sure for every pastor's wife who carries her role lovingly and faithfully, she can enjoy the delight of that adventure now if she accepts her position with confidence. For that to happen, we present ten steps for ministry spouses to follow.[5] These are adapted and expanded upon to reflect the blessings we have experienced in our marriage and ministry.

1. Embrace your calling. Remember, when God called your spouse to be a pastor, He called you, too. Trust God to use your own life just as powerfully as your spouse's to make significant contributions to His kingdom. Participate in and be a joyful part of the ministry as much as you can. Invite God to fully use you to bring much-needed hope to people in your congregation and surrounding community. It is important to have the conviction that God has called you. If you know the call is genuine and from the Lord, then you will not allow anything to deter you from that goal.

2. Know your role. You are not the church pastor. Your spouse is the one appointed to that position. Your role is that of a pastor's spouse. Your priorities are the same as they were before: God, yourself, your spouse, your family, and your church.

When church members or local leaders ask you about church matters and want your opinion, you may gently and diplomatically refer then to the pastor. People must recognize that they should address the pastor directly, and that you are not an intermediary. They must not assume that because you are the pastor's spouse, that you should know everything about church issues, whether they are benign or sensitive in nature.

3. Be a helpmate. If a wife is created to be her husband's helpmate, how much greater is this role in the case of a wife married to a pastor. The two tied in the bonds of marriage and consecrated in the calling of pastoral ministry are expected to bring to the altar all their resources of mind and spirit so that the gospel ministry can flourish and bear fruit for the glory of God and His church. As the wife, you have daily responsibilities and opportunities to help your spouse—routine chores such as laundry and cooking, and ministry concerns such as sharing his professional or spiritual burdens; or perhaps something more challenging such as conducting a seminar or even preaching occasionally. By being such a helpmate, you create a more meaningful role for yourself: you become a soulmate to your husband. His primary call as spiritual leader also embraces you, and you can now truly share and support his ministry. Even before he asks for your assistance, you can hasten to offer, "How can I help you today? Is there something you want me to do?" The same concept must be applied to the husband.

A pastor's spouse who wants to reflect God's helping character desires to sustain and uphold her husband. She will strengthen, comfort, and seek to protect him because of her love for the Lord and her husband. She leans upon the Lord for strength so that she might share that strength with her husband. In her heart he finds shelter and protection from the world; he finds a companion who offers him what he really needs: help in his God-given calling.

4. Be content. "Godliness with contentment is great gain" (1 Tim. 6:6). While the apostle Paul's counsel is applicable to all Christians, it is particularly fitting for you as a pastor's spouse. You may be under stress due to finances, church responsibilities, time demands from your family and the overall management of your home. You do it all to free your spouse to attend to ministerial duties. But if you sometimes feel unhappy and discouraged from the weight of responsibilities, your dissatisfaction will affect your family life. Go to God with your burdens believing that He can open doors to satisfy your longings and gift you with a spirit of godliness with contentment. Laying your concerns at God's throne you will be satisfied with who you are and what you have. You will turn every burden into an avenue of prayer and will find peace, joy, and fulfillment in your role as a pastor's spouse. You will be grateful for the blessings of your experience and live each day with godly courage.

> In their deportment and character will be seen the rest and peace and happiness that they have found in Jesus by daily laying their perplexities and burdens at His feet. They will show that in the path of obedience and duty there is contentment and even joy.[6]

5. Pray for your spouse. The apostle Paul instructs us to pray for one another (Eph. 6:18). His counsel is even more pertinent as you pray for the spiritual protection of your spouse and family. You should pray for them more than for anyone else. When you pray for your spouse and all the concerns and challenges of the ministry, you are able to enter into the joy of what God does for and through him.

Your spouse is the most important person in your life. You love him and want him to be all that God has called him to be. Every day your spouse faces temptations and challenges that test his commitment to the Lord. His only hope is to continually draw on the strength that God has provided. It is your responsibility to continually support him through prayer. It is worth repeating:

> The wives of ministers should live devoted, prayerful lives. . . . If they would only lean confidingly, in childlike trust, upon God, and have their affections centered in Jesus, deriving their life from Christ, the living Vine, what an amount of good they might do,

what a help they might be to others, what a support to their husbands, and what a reward would be theirs in the end![7]

6. Be a godly parent. "Children are a heritage from the Lord" (Ps. 127:3). "Jesus said, 'Let the little children come to me, and do not hinder them, for the kingdom of heaven belongs to such as these'" (Matt. 19:14). If the Word of God places such honor and value upon children, how much more should a pastor and his spouse value and cherish the children God has placed within their home.

> Minister's children are in some cases the most neglected children in the world, for the reason that the father is with them but little, and they are left to choose their own employment and amusement. . . . Let the minister's wife who has children remember that in her home she has a missionary field in which she should labor with untiring energy and unflagging zeal, knowing that the results of her work will endure throughout eternity. . . . then let her tend them with loving care. She is charged with the responsibility of showing to the world the power and excellence of home religion. She is to be controlled by principle, not by impulse, and she is to work with the consciousness that God is her helper. She is to allow nothing to divert her from her mission.[8]

In light of such counsel, what should the pastor's spouse do to care for their children? First and foremost, love them with all seriousness and sacredness that God expects you to bestow on the precious trust He has given to you both. Love them because they are God's gift to you and God holds you accountable.

Expecting your children to be perfect just because a parent is a pastor is both unrealistic and unfair. Let them know that their parent's calling and ministry is important, but that they are not responsible for the success or failure of the family's ministry. At the same time show them by precept and example that they are accountable to God. Tell them that your love for them is unconditional and to treasure Christ as their friend. When they err, teach them that God's grace and love are sufficient to overcome all deficiencies, and encourage them to keep growing closer to Christ in whom they can trust and confide.

7. Use your spiritual gifts. Focus on what God has gifted you to do rather than trying to do too much and losing your effectiveness. Think and pray about what you most enjoy doing and what you do especially well.

Thus you will discover your spiritual gifts. The more you focus in these gifts, utilizing them in the service of God, the sooner you will discover your true identity as a follower of Christ and pastor's spouse. In that discovery, you will find freedom from external pressures, meaningless competitions, and doubts about your self-worth. Only then will you be fully equipped and spiritually mature to serve God as He created you to be.

8. Make friends. True friends play an important role in life. They share your sorrows, laugh with you, listen to your woes, counsel you when need it, and pray with and for you. When true friends point out your faults it is because they love you and are there to help. They cheer you up when you are down and offer you a fresh perspective on life. They are there to love, care for, and support you. That is who true friends are.

While most people have such special friends, and while you also may have them, as a pastor's spouse be sure you do not give the impression that you prefer the company of one over others. A pastor's spouse must be a friend to all—that is, anyone in your congregation who needs a helping hand, needs a listening ear, or needs to talk. The pastor and his spouse must be seen as being open to such needs. The friendships you build are valuable in strengthening the fellowship of the church. Accept invitations to social events whenever possible. Keep in mind that, as a pastor's spouse, you are an example of faith and love in action. Avoid playing favorites; instead live with grace, integrity, and fairness.

9. Value intimacy in your marriage. Intimacy is about being emotionally close to your spouse. Be absolutely open and free, letting him know how you really feel. Intimacy is also about accepting and sharing feelings, being there when the other needs you. Share your "inner world" with the one you love, including your whole range of feelings and experiences—pain and sadness, happiness and love.

Most of us, however, find it easier to share some feelings more than others. For example, are you both able to let each other know how you feel about the other? Saying "I love you" is important. Assuming your partner knows of your love because of the way you behave is not enough. Intimacy in marriage does not happen by magic. It must be built over time. For some this takes longer than others. Often the harder you work at intimacy, the more valuable and rewarding it is. Be positive about what you have in your relationship and let your husband know what you value about him and your relationship. Everyone likes to be told that they are appreciated and loved.

It is thrilling to hear wonderful things over and over. Ellen G. White expands on Psalm 24:7-10, saying all heaven awaits to "welcome the Saviour to the celestial courts. . . . Joyfully the waiting sentinels respond, 'Who is the Kind of glory?' This they say, not because they know not who He is, but because they would hear the answer of exalted praise. . ."[9] Likewise, hearing that we are loved and being encouraged to excel is a healing balm for the soul. Never tire of gifting the words "I love you" to your beloved.

Create opportunities for intimacy. Make time to be alone and focus on each other and your relationship. If this is hard to do because of children, work, or other commitments, find ways to fulfill the need for closeness and intimacy. Its importance cannot be overemphasized.

"Love cannot long exist without expression. Let not the heart of one connected with you starve for the want of kindness and sympathy. . . . the love that binds heart to heart, is a foretaste of the joys of heaven."[10]

10. Love people. One of the truly remarkable qualities that must characterize a ministry couple is their abiding commitment to truly love the members they serve. There is a special anointing upon the pastor's spouse to go beyond the normal call of duty. As much as possible, express your love to each one in your church with neither favor nor partiality. You can do it by following up on their requests for prayer, talking with them about their concerns, authentically sharing your struggles, socializing with everyone equally, serving through acts of kindness, giving them unconditional love when they have failed, welcoming them with hugs, ministering to them in crises, learning and remembering their names, being available to them, and taking a genuine interest in their lives.

It is important to understand that being a pastor's spouse is not the same as being a church member. Your role brings different challenges and opportunities in your life. "The wife of a minister can do much if she will. If she possesses the spirit of self-sacrifice, and has a love for souls, she can with him do almost an equal amount of good."[11] Moreover, she will certainly have a meaningful and blessed life, maintaining a happy and exemplary Christian life and family, with all its promised joys and eternal rewards.

BIBLICAL LIGHT FOR THE PASTORAL SPOUSE

The Bible does not give any specific job description for a pastor's spouse, although it speaks about the character and duties of a virtuous woman (Prov. 31:10–31), a Christian wife and mother (Eph. 5), and the older women's role as mentors to younger women (Titus 2:3–5). This lack of specific instruction does not mean that a pastor's spouse is free from responsibilities to the congregation. On the contrary, it should be taken to mean that we are left to infer the role and character of a pastor's spouse from what the Scriptures teach about women in general, and their role in the family and community as a wife and believer. The absence of specific instructions regarding a pastor's wife may indeed be taken positively. While a pastor's wife is not expected to play a specific role, she should be seen as a solid supporter of her husband in his varied ministerial duties; and also in the life of the congregation, particularly for female members who may seek her counsel, prayer, or just some encouragement in their time of need. As a pastor's wife, the opportunities for her to strengthen the faith of her fellow believers, especially women, are limitless.

So, as a pastoral spouse, consider yourself first and foremost a person called to be a helpmate to the pastor and parent of your children. Nowhere does the Word of God indicate that you belong to a special class of people, but everything in Scripture, particularly on the interrelationship and responsibility within God's fellowship, teaches about your unique identity, role, and purpose as a woman, and by extension your position as a pastor's spouse.

> A sister laborer in the cause of truth can understand and reach some cases, especially among the sisters, that the minister cannot. A responsibility rests upon the minister's wife which she should not and cannot lightly throw off. God will require the talent lent her, with usury. She should work earnestly, faithfully, and unitedly with her husband to save souls.[12]

PASTOR'S SPOUSE: TRADITIONAL AND CONTEMPORARY MODELS

Traditional model. There was a time when the church had an idealistic, or unrealistic, view of the role of the pastor's wife. That concept held that the "ideal" wife of the pastor must possess certain essential characteristics that would help her fulfill her role. While many of those characteristics were of value then, and still are today, women were not perceived as individuals with different personalities and backgrounds and who needed to be themselves—not mass produced same mold.

Leonard I. Sweet, in his book *The Minister's Wife: Her Role in Nineteenth-Century American Evangelicalism*, identified four roles of the traditional pastor's wife:[13]

1. The companion. The pastor's wife is a "ministering angel" to her husband and takes care of all of his needs and upholding his sacred calling.

2. The sacrificer. She cares for the home and all aspects of ministry life so that her husband's call to the ministry of the church is hindered. She asks very little of him "by staying out of his way and raising the family on her own."

3. The assistant. She helps with her husband's pastoral responsibilities and becomes her husband's right arm, sharing many pastoral duties and functioning as an extension of his ministry.

4. The partner. She shares the ministry with her husband by doing her part in the ministry. In a way, she became the pastor's pastor whenever he needs encouragement and spiritual support.

This traditional model of the past that set the standard or mandate for pastor's wives is still used in many places. It hints of a pastoral wife's unworthiness as an individual unless she has a high spirit of sacrifice and service, not only for her husband, but also for God.[14] Many women who accept this traditional role take the innate burdens of such a view upon themselves,—in many ways trying to be the perfect example they were expected to be—never wanting anyone to see the ministerial couple in a negative light. In this model, the pastor's wife is "'put on a pedestal' by the congregation to be admired and imitated in what she does and how she does it."[15]

Contemporary model. A second model is more recent. According to Susie Hawkins, this contemporary model was developed towards the end of the twentieth century. The pattern is based on contemporary church culture and is what the new generation of ministry wives are looking to model.[16]

Here pastoral wives are comfortable with who they are and have authentic interactions with parishioners. They build relationships with them based on friendship, community, and common goals. They display qualities of transparency, common experiences, and honest conversation.[17]

Many pastors' wives in the contemporary model follow Sweet's 3rd and 4th roles—assistant or partner in her husband's ministry. They do not limit themselves to solely tending to their household needs. They are actively involved in the ministry of the church and, laboring according to their own God-given talents, share in their husband's responsibilities as a pastor.[18]

There is no handbook for the contemporary pastoral wife. But one thing is clear, she does not do the work of the pastor. Rather, she offers her energy and abilities and becomes a ministerial team with her husband, glad to be yoked together with him to do God's work.

Her role as a pastor's wife is not just to play the piano, labor in church as other member do, or to lead the women's ministries. If she enjoys playing the piano or leading out the women, so be it. But her main role in the church and the life of the pastor is to be there for him as his partner in life and ministry. She shares his burdens, feels his disappointments, suffers his defeats, and stands by him through thick and thin. She often reviews his sermons, offering constructive criticism. She is discrete, encouraging, an attentive listener, and a wise counselor. The same concept is valid for a husband when the pastor is a woman.

A pastor's wife heals her husband's emotional wounds and cheers him on. She is quick to discern difficulties that may arise, which her husband does not yet perceive. She loves, protects, and shields him from pain when the burdens of pastoring threaten to dampen his spirit. Pastoral work can be a lonely profession. Many pastors do not have close friends in whom they can confide. But his wife is privileged in that she can fill that role. In fact, she is his oasis, his God-given haven.

Finally, she bravely tackles on her supreme duties, being a trustworthy wife and mother. But hers is a life of prayer, and she leans on the everlasting arms of the Almighty. This is how she is able to shoulder the demands of home and ministry.

PASTORAL SPOUSE: PRESSING ONWARD AND UPWARD

While being a pastor's spouse is truly a remarkable calling, the success of this mission depends on your commitment and devotion to the ministry. "A truly converted woman will exert a powerful transforming influence for good. Connected with her husband, she may aid him in his work, and become the means of encouragement and blessing to him. When the will and way are brought into subjection to the Spirit of God, there is no limit to the good that can be accomplished."[19]

To keep yourself motivated and focused, here are some suggestions from Raquel, who has walked in the path of ministry for years and has experienced both joys and challenges.

Don't feel discouraged. Congregations often compare the current pastor's wife with the former pastor's wife. Such comparisons can be intimidating and discouraging. But be patient. They need time to get to know you—so be yourself, and set your own objectives and plan how you will achieve them. Love the people, win them over, and create change slowly. You are your own person, and you need to find your own way. This can be done with grace and gentle determination. Your success depends on how comfortable you are with yourself and on your reliance on God to guide your destiny.

Be yourself. Do not allow others to define your role or set your goals, "People often place the pastor and his family on a pedestal. It is good that others show respect for the office of pastor, but people need to see that you are also human and real. People are looking for realness, both spiritually as well as personally."[20] Shannon L. Alder rightly says, "One of the greatest regrets in life is being what others would want you to be, rather than being yourself."

Our true self is who we are when we let go of all of the stories, labels, and judgments that we have placed upon ourselves. It is our natural self without the mask and pretentiousness.

Stimulate respect for him. A pastor's wife should add value to her husband as a person and minister, and encourage others to be courteous to him and treat him with dignity. She does this by intentionally emulating that herself, thus showing respect for him and support for his work. However, some congregations are more challenging to deal with and you may need to raise your game a notch. Therefore, when speaking about your husband, avoid referring to him as "my husband" or "John" (supposing his name is John Smith). Rather, refer to him as "Pr. Smith" or "the pastor" or "our pastor." In so doing, you are affirming the respect his position deserves.

Let him be a professional. Pastoring is a professional just like any other profession—teachers, doctors, accountants, etc.—and a pastor is expected to perform his duties in a professional manner. Be it tending to an office, relating to the church board, meeting with church members, visiting the sick, being available for counseling, running a nominating committee, the pastor is expected to be professional. These functions take time and require scheduling. Therefore, a pastor's wife should not assume that her husband is free to be with her at home or run errands for her anytime she pleases.

Some wives may think that the pastor is his own boss and has flexible schedule. But such an assumption does not respect the professionalism and time-conscious nature of ministry. A pastor's wife should support her husband by letting him be a professional in his work. Secular work demands high standards of professionalism and diligence, how much more then should we give due diligence to God's work.

Effective ministry is hard work and takes a toll on the amount of time the couple has to dedicate to each other. Many wives resent this. The remedy is for her to consider ministry as their combined work and not the pastor's work alone. Team ministry is the answer. It is accomplished through collaboration. A pastoral wife who assumes ownership in ministry can accept her husband's commitment to professionalism. She will move forward accomplishing her own responsibilities in ministry. And the harmony of their united efforts will be a blessing to both God's cause and their own marriage.

Be an encourager. "Encourage one another" is Paul's counsel to all believers (2 Cor. 13:11). How much more should a pastoral couple encourage and support each other. As an encourager, a pastor's wife listens to her husband's joyful experiences and burdensome challenges. She praises God for her husband's achievements of the day and place him before God in earnest prayer for the discouragements he may have faced during the day. And she affirms him with her confidence in his ministry, offering her unreserved support. The more often she says, "I love you. You can do it. I believe in you," the more his spiritual batteries and emotional reserves will get recharged. He should know that, next to God, his unfailing source of support is his godly wife.

> They [pastoral wives] can cheer them when desponding, comfort them when cast down, and encourage them to look up and trust fully in God when their faith fails. Or they can take an opposite course, look upon the dark side, think they have a hard time, exercise no faith in God, talk their trials and unbelief to their companions, indulge a complaining, murmuring spirit, and be a dead weight and even a curse to them.[21]

God desires that pastoral spouses not make the mistake of taking the "opposite course," but rather be true enablers and Spirit-filled encouragers of their spouse's ministry. As a thankful pastor once remarked, "When my wife encourages me, I feel like there's nothing I can't do! There's no mountain I can't climb or a problem I can't solve. Nothing energizes a pastor more than having a sense of fulfillment in serving God and that he has the encouragement and support of his wife."

Take care of him. As one married to the same man for over three decades, I have no hesitation in saying that the biblical concept of marriage makes the two of us responsible for each other—in love, caring, helping, meeting each other's needs, raising our family, and the absolute certainty that we have each other for the rest of our lives. I am a special and unique strength to my husband, who happens to be a pastor. That helping ministry extends to everything from caring for his wardrobe, medical checkups, and special appointments, to timely expressions of appreciation and suggestions that would benefit his pastoral role.

Yes, I hear some pastor's wives respond saying, "What about me? Why is it all about him!" Well, this section of the book is about him—how to add value to your husband, worth to his calling, and meaning to his mission. Perhaps it is time that you ask yourself: Has my husband found in me the fulfillment of the promise given in Proverbs 18:22—"He who finds a wife finds what is good and receives favor from the Lord?" Am I transmitting the excellence and graciousness of God to his ministry so that he can share with those to whom he ministers the light and strength that flow from the Lord? Does he consider me as a favor received from the Lord? In what sense am I a favor? Do I continually lift him and his ministry before the throne of grace? Am I a praying, faithful wife who trusts in God and believes that the ministry my husband is called to perform is truly a favor from the Lord?

CONCLUSION

Love and faith, prayer and grace, must flow from the sanctuary of your soul, so your husband can indeed say that he has found a woman of great worth and extraordinary value. He "trusts her without reserve, and never has reason to regret it" (Prov. 31:11, *The Message*). And "she treats him generously all her life long" (v. 12). He finds her "worth far more than rubies" and "has full confidence in her" (vv. 10, 11).

"The wife of a minister of the gospel can be either a most successful helper and a great blessing to her husband or a hindrance to him in his work. It depends very much on the wife whether a minister will rise from day to day in his sphere of usefulness, or whether he will sink to the ordinary level."[22]

What kind of a pastor's wife are you? You don't have to be involved in many ministries to have an impact as a role model, mentor, and example of what it means to be a Christian woman and wife. Being a pastoral wife means being yourself and being comfortable with yourself, knowing that God made you unique and that He has a purpose and plan for your life. Once you discover that purpose and plan through a life of prayer, meditation, study of God's Word, and single-minded devotion to God's service and your husband's ministry, you will discover the unlimited potential of your own spiritual gifts. Only then can you confidently minister to those who come within the sphere of your fellowship and your husband's ministry. Together your husband and you will experience the fullness of the power of ministry. And your church will call you blessed.

QUESTIONS FOR REFLECTION OR DISCUSSION

1. What do you think is your most important responsibility as a pastoral spouse?
2. What do you think is not part of your role, even though others may assume it is?
3. What boundaries have you established to protect your marriage and family life?
4. How do you define your role as a pastor's spouse?
5. How do you add value to your husband's life and ministry?

ENDNOTES

1   Sarah Jane Wessels, "Care for the Pastor's Wife, Too!" *Ministry Health*, no. 219 (1998), last modified October 5, 2004, http://www.ministryhealth.net/mh_articles/219_sv_care_pastors_wife.html, accessed March 14, 2009.

2   Ellen G. White, *Testimonies for the Church* (Mountain View, CA: Pacific Press, 1948), 1:453.

3   Gayle Haggard, "Special Encouragement for the Pastor's Wife," in *Leading Women to the Heart of God*, ed. Lysa TerKeurst (Chicago, IL: Moody Publishers, 2002), 255.

4   White, *Testimonies for the Church*, 1:452, 453.

5   This section includes information adapted from Lisa McKay, *You Can Still Wear Cute Shoes, and Other Great Advice From an Unlikely Preacher's Wife* (Colorado Springs: David C. Cook, 2010).

6   White, *Counsels to Parents, Teachers, and Students* (Mountain View, CA: Pacific Press, 1913), 98.

7   See note 4.

8   White, *Gospel Workers* (Washington, DC: Review and Herald, 1915), 206.

9   White, *The Desire of Ages* (Mountain View, CA: Pacific Press, 1940), 833.

10   White, *The Ministry of Healing* (Mountain View, CA: Pacific Press, 1942), 360.

11   White, *Evangelism* (Washington, DC: Review and Herald, 1946), 675.

12   White, *Testimonies for the Church*, 1:452.

13   Adapted from Debra D. Benoit, "The Changing Role of the Pastor's Wife in Today's Evangelical Church" (DMin thesis, Liberty Baptist Theological Seminary, 2010), 15, 16, http://digitalcommons.liberty.edu/cgi/viewcontent.cgi?article=1446&-context=doctoral, with some quotations from Leonard I. Sweet, *The Minister's Wife: Her Role in Nineteenth-Century American Evangelicalism* (Philadelphia, PA: Temple University Press, 1983), 3, accessed March 12, 2015.

14   Adapted from Benoit, "Changing Role of the Pastor's Wife," 16.

15   Adapted from Benoit, "Changing Role of the Pastor's Wife," 20, with quotation from Susie Hawkins, *From One Ministry Wife to Another* (Chicago, IL: Moody Publishers, 2009), 28.

16   Adapted from Benoit, "Changing Role of the Pastor's Wife," 21, with quotation from Hawkins, *From One Ministry Wife to Another*, 25.

17   Adapted from Benoit, "Changing Role of the Pastor's Wife," 21; Hawkins, *From One Ministry Wife to Another*, 25.

18   Adapted from Benoit, "Changing Role of the Pastor's Wife," 22; Sweet, *The Minister's Wife*, 3.

19   White, *Evangelism*, 467, 468.

20   "Role of a Pastor's Wife," Pastoral Care, Inc., http://www.pastoralcareinc.com/articles/role-of-a-pastor-s-wife/, accessed July 15, 2016.

21   White, *Testimonies for the Church*, 1:139.

22   White, *The Adventist Home* (Nashville, TN: Southern Publishing, 1952), 355.

— CHAPTER 5 —

THE PASTOR'S CHALLENGES

"When God comes in His fullness, then our ministry will become easy, it will be a blessing and a pleasure, not a load and a burden."—Sunday Adelaja

What a great privilege it is to be a pastor and co-laborer with Jesus. It is a good thing to desire to serve God as shepherd in His church. "If a man desires the position of a bishop, he desires a good work" (1 Tim. 3:1, NKJV). By tending the flock of God, pastors become instruments of mercy in God's hands. They work to enlarge the kingdom of God, and no other obligation is a nobler calling or a higher honor. Pastors bear the good news of salvation to a lost world. The sick and suffering seek them for empathy. And as they share the blessed hope with the world, God's saving grace gives them immense joy, blessing their life beyond compare.

By being pastors, they embrace the gifts and talents God has given them and use them every day on behalf of His people and to His glory. Pastoring is a wonderful vocation. Yet, it carries with it great responsibilities, none of which are to be taken lightly. But with a firm determination, unwavering commitment, and the guidance of the Spirit of God, pastors can claim victory over many difficulties that will challenge their ministry.

CHALLENGES IN PASTORAL MINISTRY

There are important and significant moments in ministry. Many are joyous, but some are not. Unfortunately, at times pastors may feel ambushed by challenges.

The dedication of pastors moves them to listen to those experiencing grief and discouragement. With a caring spirit they suffer when unable to help people in need because of lack of time or resources. Patiently they put up with gossip and bickering among parishioners. And their love for Christ help them endure criticism and gossip about their competence. But they feel often appreciated and are unable to meet all the needs, as well as all the demands within their own families.

How can pastors satisfy all of their obligations and expectations? In life, people experience joys and face challenges, and it is not any different for those involved in ministry. In this chapter we will discuss a few challenges pastors and church leaders may face.

COMMUNION WITH GOD

Due to the complexities of life, communion with God has become a big challenge for many pastors and church leaders. Yet, a healthy spiritual life, involving a deep and abiding relationship with God, is their greatest need. Pastors cannot fulfill their calling without this. Do not undermine the cultivation of a vibrant spiritual life. Walk daily with God and manifest deep caring and love for His flock. Ellen G. White confirms this: "The reason why our preachers accomplish so little is that they do not walk with God. He is a day's journey from most of them."[1] Hence, if a pastor does not cultivate and sustain a daily personal relationship with God, his influence and example of godliness will fall short of excellence.

For this reason, pastors, we urge you to fall in love with the Word of God; meditate upon it; talk to God in prayer as often as possible; place all of your burdens upon Him and be specific; set aside definite time slots to worship Him in solitude, and ask Him to be your guide and guardian for the duties of the day. It is imperative that you do this so you receive strength and wisdom from the Holy Spirit to be a blessing in the lives of others. "We need to look constantly to Jesus, realizing that it is His power which does the work. While we are to labor earnestly for the salvation of the lost, we must also take time for meditation, for prayer, and for the study of the word of God. Only the work accomplished with much prayer, and sanctified by the merit of Christ, will in the end prove to have been efficient for good."[2]

What gives my ministry its joy, motivation, and strength, is the time I dedicate to my devotional life, my time alone with God. When I daily admit how needy I am, meditate on the grace of the Lord Jesus Christ, and feed on the restorative wisdom of His Word, I am propelled to share with others the grace that I receive. To obtain all of this, there are no pastoral or leadership skills available, nor any instructions manual, only the study of the Bible and being in the presence of God.

It is also my personal worship time that enables me to lead others to worship God as well. My sense of need leads me to tenderly pastor those also in need of grace. My study of God's Word guides me in sharing the right

Word of counsel and direction with others. My joy in Christ inspires others to rejoice in Christ. When I am "in Christ" it is easier to speak about and lead others to be "in Christ." Such is also Paul's counsel: "I have become all things to all people so that by all possible means I might save some" (1 Cor. 9:22).

FAMILY CONCERNS

As a pastor, I have come to understand that one of the greatest failures in ministry is the lack of discipline to be present, especially where the family is concerned. Ministry often takes priority over family care, but a well-disciplined pastor must find a balance between ministry time and family time. Being in the same room or eating at the same dinner table does not qualify as being present. Failure to be present is failure to really live.[3]

> Nothing can excuse the minister for neglecting the inner circle for the larger circle outside. The spiritual welfare of his family comes first. In the day of final reckoning, God will inquire what he did to win to Christ those whom he took the responsibility of bringing into the world. Great good done for others cannot cancel the debt that he owes to God to care for his own children.[4]

We know that a pastor's work often takes him out of the home. It can be emotionally draining without quality family time. Even when pastors are physically at home, their minds may be miles away. Feeling their duty to the church supersedes all family responsibilities, they may even risk becoming workaholics. But their families need them. "The minister's duties lie around him, nigh and afar off; but his first duty is to his children. . . . The world is not so much in need of great minds, as of good men, who are a blessing in their home."[5]

God, family, and ministry, in that order, are the crucial priorities in the life of a pastor. While we are to fear, love, trust, and serve God as our first and foremost priority, the concern remains: what about the other two?

The Adventist church outlined the pastoral job description as it relates to the expectations of congregations and conferences.[6] But pastors are also accountable to their own families and their needs and expectations. They must not consider think ministerial duties take precedence over family responsibilities. If a pastor always and deliberately assigns more importance to ministry over family responsibility, how will he or she justify these choices before God on that final day of reckoning? When inquired of pastors, "Where is the flock that was given to you" (Jer. 13:20, NKJV), how will pastors answer?

Pastor, be present at home. You and your spouse are God's two pillars of spiritual support. Do not undermine the position assigned to you the day God created humanity. The shoes of spiritual stewardship are to be filled by both parents. "Woman should fill the position which God originally assigned for her, as her husband's equal."[7] Yet, that does not mean that your spouse should be left alone to fill both spiritual roles just because she is spiritually capable of carrying out hers effectively. And that does not excuse you as a father from having a latent spiritual presence in your home. In many homes around the globe and throughout the centuries, the absence of men in family life has made it necessary to emphasize fatherhood. God forbid that should be the case in the home of a pastor! Ministers who are never around because of church work and expect spouses to pick up the slack, are in essence evading and diminishing their spiritual influence in the lives of their children.

Chapter 1 discusses the three-strand cord in ministry: Jesus, you, and your spouse. This victorious trio also holds true in your home. You may have the assurance that Jesus oversees your family. You may be thankful that your godly spouse steps up to the plate. But pastor, what about you? Your presence, influence, and involvement, are summoned. You are part of the equation. You are watched by your children, your spouse, and your church members. Therefore, be accountable, because God will ask you: "Where is the flock that was given to you?" At that time, may both you and your spouse reply in unison, and with confidence: "Here we are with the children you gave us."

FINANCIAL LIMITATIONS

Finances often pose serious challenges for pastors in many places. Such challenges include the inability to provide a decent living for their family; insufficient funds for household needs in times of low pay and high inflation; lack of adequate savings for emergencies and retirement; and pressure on spouses to seek employment, which, in turn, increases the need for their involvement in housekeeping and running errands. All of this affects the time pastors spend in ministry.

According to Dr. Ryan Howes, financial stress can affect thoughts, feelings, and behavior.[8] It can hinder motivation and performance. More than that, when people are paid inadequately, they tend to focus on the unfairness of the situation, allowing bitterness and resentment surface.

People are motivated by money. While money does not buy happiness, everybody seems to want to discover for themselves whether that is true or not. So being short of money often results in people doing whatever it takes to get more in order to be happy and satisfied. But for the Christian, and definitely for pastors, having a meaningful life should take precedence over wealth because God knows our situation and assures us, "Look at the birds of the air . . . your heavenly Father feeds them. Are you not much more valuable than they? . . . But seek first his kingdom and his righteousness, and all these things will be given to you as well" (Mat. 6:26, 33)

Financial stability can help dissipate stress, while being overwhelmed by financial worries foments doubt. What is pastors to do when money issues threaten the welfare of their families? Know that God is in complete control. Believe that He will come through. And exercise your faith by observing disciplines that can keep in check critical challenges in family finances. Here are a few suggestions.

- *Pray.* A pastoral family that prays together finds strength for and assistance in unusual sources. They claim the promise that "God shall supply all your need according to His riches in glory by Christ Jesus" (Phil. 4:19, NKJV).
- *Prepare a family budget.* Involve all family members, focusing on your income, estimated expenses, and needs. Strictly follow a budget. Resist the temptation to spend on what is not budgeted. Writing to a family living beyond its means, White said, "If you would learn the lesson of economy and see the peril to yourselves and to your children and to the cause of God in this free use of means, you would obtain an experience essential to the perfection of your Christian character. Unless you do obtain such an experience, your children will bear the mold of a defective education as long as they live."[9]
- *Practice economy.* "If you have extravagant habits, cut them away from your life at once. Unless you do this, you will be bankrupt for eternity. Habits of economy, industry, and sobriety are a better portion for your children than a rich dowry."[10]
- *Restrict your wants.* "We are pilgrims and strangers on the earth. Let us not spend our means in gratifying desires that God would have us repress. Let us fitly represent our faith by restricting our wants."[11]
- *Remember God provides.* God never lets His people down. The experience of the psalmist can be yours: "I was young and now I am old, yet I have never seen the righteous forsaken or their children begging bread" (Ps. 37:25). As it was with the psalmist, the Lord is your shepherd, and you shall not want (Ps. 23:1).

Those who obey the Lord's calling in faith and enter the ministry have nothing to fear. God will supply all their needs. Therefore, seek contentment;

it dissipates greed and covetousness. Contentment comes from humbly accepting the lifestyle provided to you. "I have learned to be content in whatever circumstances I am. I know how to get along with humble means, and I also know how to live in prosperity; in any and every circumstance I have learned the secret of being filled and going hungry, both of having abundance and suffering need" (Phil. 4:11, 12, NASB).

On the other hand, we cannot ignore the fact that in some places pastors are not receiving a fair wage. Ellen G. White comments:

> The displeasure of God is kindled against those who claim to be His followers, yet allow consecrated workers to suffer for the necessities of life while engaged in active ministry. These selfish ones will be called to render an account, not only for the misuse of their Lord's money, but for the depression and heartache which their course has brought upon His faithful servants. Those who are called to the work of the ministry, and at the call of duty give up all to engage in God's service, should receive for their self-sacrificing efforts wages sufficient to support themselves and their families.[12]

"In the various departments of secular labor, mental and physical, faithful workmen can earn good wages. Is not the work of disseminating truth, and leading souls to Christ, of more importance than any ordinary business? And are not those who faithfully engage in this work justly entitled to ample remuneration? By our estimate of the relative value of labor for moral and for physical good, we show our appreciation of the heavenly in contrast with the earthly."[13]

TIME CONSTRAINTS

Ministry responsibilities are not confined to regular business hours. Pastors are on duty twenty-four hours a day, seven days a week. They frequently receive phone calls throughout the day, and often in the middle of the night. Most of their home activities, social calls, and relationships are related to the church. Even conversations within the family or among friends revolve around church matters in one way or another. Their homes, which should be a refuge from labor and a place of rest from ministerial cares and concerns, often lose their privacy and become an extension of the workplace. Pastoral obligations are continuous and pastors are often drained of energy with no place to hide from ministerial duties and concerns.

To be efficient and successful in ministry, pastors would do well to learn time management and carefully utilize their time. All of us, have the same amount of time. The only difference in the way we manage our time. Work out a system that meets all of the needs of your family and ministry. When your time is managed in a systematic manner, you will not run short of it or face incomplete tasks at the end of the day.

> Our time belongs to God. Every moment is His, and we are under the most solemn obligation to improve it to His glory. Of no talent He has given will He require a more strict account than of our time. The value of time is beyond computation. . . . Life is too short to be trifled away. We have but a few days of probation in which to prepare for eternity. We have no time to waste, no time to devote to selfish pleasure, no time for the indulgence of sin.[14]

Paul's counsel is timely: "Be careful then how you live, not as unwise people but as wise, making the most of the time" (Eph. 5:15, 16, NRSV). Jonathan Edwards, a renowned preacher of the eighteenth century, wrote this resolution on his twentieth birthday: "Resolved, Never to lose one moment of time, but to improve it in the most profitable way I possibly can." And he did, and rose to be an effective and influential pastor in his day. To live as a Christian is to live with a sense of time.

CONFLICT AND CRITICISM

Conflict and criticism are common in churches. They are Satan's weapon of choice to harm the church's soul-sustaining and soul-winning objectives. "Believers have not infrequently allowed the enemy to work through them . . . Cherishing a spirit of criticism and faultfinding, of pharisaical piety and pride, they have grieved away the Spirit of God and have greatly retarded the work of God's messengers."[15]

How should pastors react to this? Ignore destructive and unfavorable comments, or confront the accusers who sow discontent?

Much criticism is due to differences of opinion involving differences in culture and aesthetic taste and preferences, when in fact fellowship and unity of the church are more important than any peripheral concerns. "Yoking up with Christ, learning His meekness and lowliness, cuts short many a conflict; for when the enemy comes in like a flood, the Spirit of the Lord lifts up a standard against him."[16]

Worse than petty complaints, is church members unjustly criticizing pastors. It was no different for the apostles of Christ; they contended with prejudice and even hatred. But pastor, do not allow this to drive you to despair, discouragement, or bitterness. Only consider truths, if any, that may be hidden in such criticism, correct your ways if necessary, and move on. But do not partake of their foolishness, and ignore their cruel remarks.

> The precious Saviour will send help just when we need it. The way to heaven is consecrated by His footprints. Every thorn that wounds our feet has wounded His. Every cross that we are called to bear He has borne before us. The Lord permits conflicts, to prepare the soul for peace.[17]

However, when false accusations go beyond a personal attack against the pastor and inhibits the advancement of the gospel, it is time to take action. The builders of the house of God in Nehemiah's day labored with one hand and held on to a weapon with the other (Neh. 4:17). Your weapon is to confront your accusers and stop them in their tracks. Asking them for proof will usually stop them because their discontent is usually borne out of unfounded gossip. Dear pastor, bring glory and honor to God by defending His cause. Then continue being like a builder of the temple, "with unfaltering faith and unfailing courage." [18]

LACK OF COMMITMENT

Apathy, indifference, and a lack of commitment to what the church is and what it expects of the believers often pose a real challenge to pastoral ministry and leadership. Even though the problem may not be widespread, when commitment is not perceived within a congregation, much harm can come to the worship, fellowship, witness, and growth of the church. Consider and learn from the early church in the book of Acts. The secret of their speedy growth was their unified, Spirit-filled, unreserved commitment to their Lord and His mission: "All the believers were together and had everything in common. . . . Every day they continued to meet together in the temple courts. They broke bread in their homes and ate together with glad and sincere hearts" (Acts 2:44–46).

With such spiritual oneness and commitment, the apostolic church experienced the power of the Spirit. It can be the same today,

It is not because of any restriction on the part of God that the riches of His grace do not flow earthward to men. If the fulfillment of the promise is not seen as it might be, it is because the promise is not appreciated as it should be. If all were willing, all would be filled with the Spirit.[19]

Two principles can help pastors and church leaders guide their churches toward greater accomplishment of God's assigned objectives:

1. Understand the mission of the church. The mission of the church today remains the same as it was when Christ established the church while He was here on earth. The church is the body of Christ with a defined mission to worship, study, fellowship, and proclaim the message of the saving grace, sanctifying power, and soon return of Jesus Christ.

The church is God's appointed agency for the salvation of men. It was organized for service, and its mission is to carry the gospel to the world. From the beginning it has been God's plan that through His church shall be reflected to the world His fullness and His sufficiency. The members of the church, those whom He has called out of darkness into His marvelous light, are to show forth His glory. The church is the repository of the riches of the grace of Christ.[20]

2. Understand the philosophy of ministry. A thorough knowledge of the biblical philosophy of ministry will help pastors and parishioners to understand and be fully involved in the varied aspects of ministry. It can be found in various places in Scripture, including the Great Commission: "Therefore go and make disciples of all nations, baptizing them in the name of the Father and of the Son and of the Holy Spirit, and teaching them to obey everything I have commanded you. And surely I am with you always, to the very end of the age" (Matt. 28:19, 20). The Commission underscores four basic principles of Christian ministry.

- *First*, ministers are called in the name of the Father, Son, and Holy Spirit. Ministry is the mission of the entire Godhead. They maintain their vital connection to God through the study of His Word and constant communion in prayer (2 Tim. 2:15; Acts 6:4). They must personally know the Lord of the Cross and the Resurrection (Gal. 6:14; 1 Cor. 15:8). Without an abiding relationship with Jesus— heart to heart, mind to mind—no one can be part of His ministry

(John 15:4). Constant fellowship with Him is a prerequisite for ministers who desire to be active and ongoing witnesses for Jesus. They must be spiritual to receive the power of the Spirit (John 20:21, 22; 16:13–15).

- *Second,* ministry is taking the saving message of the gospel to all peoples and to make disciples of all nations (Eph. 2:14), for God is no respecter of persons, He shows no favoritism (Acts 10:34, 35).
- *Third,* ministry is teaching what Jesus has commanded and ensuring it is faithfully observed.
- *Fourth,* ministry is baptizing and preparing a people for the end of time when Chris returns to take us to His Father's home (John 14:1–3).

Go, teach, baptize, make disciples—that is ministry in a nutshell.

When your congregation discovers and commits itself to such a mission and ministry, there will be little room for lethargy and triviality. A lazy mind, it is said, is the workshop of the devil. In the context of our discussion, we might say, "A church that fails to understand the mission and what directs the ministry is a center for apathy and indifference." So, pastors, encourage your people to discover their mission and role in the church and to find fulfillment within that pattern. Only then will they, as a church, be happy and satisfied.

God takes men as they are, and educates them for His service, if they will yield themselves to Him. . . . The weak, vacillating character becomes changed to one of strength and steadfastness. Continual devotion establishes so close a relation between Jesus and His disciple that the Christian becomes like Him in mind and character.[21]

LACK OF MOTIVATION

Without proper motivation and a yearning to nurture and serve the Lord's flock, a ministry could suffer and lack what is needed for the growth. Even the pastor himself could feel a sting of discouragement because he lacks the power of right motivation. What should happen? "A desire to glorify God should be to us the most powerful of all motives. It should lead us to make every exertion to improve the privileges and opportunities provided for us, to use wisely the Lord's goods. It should lead us to keep brain, bone, and muscle in the most healthful condition, that our physical strength and mental clearness may help us to be faithful stewards."[22]

Where motivation is lacking, pastors may lose the desire to minister. Their will and drive to engage in Spirit-oriented ministry recedes like the sea from the shore, and their pastoral work does not reflect the urgency of God's Word on fire. In other words, ministry without proper motivation takes its toll on ministers to the point of not caring whether they ever preach again with pastoral care, biblical authority, or ministerial urgency. Such situations often lead to depression and a neglect of pastoral concerns. Signs of major depression are a lack of drive and energy in performing ministerial duties, being withdrawn and not wanting to be around others, having a tendency to sleep often, getting into quarrels or confrontations with others over insignificant issues, and so forth.

When pastors face such signs of negative feelings, they should take positive steps to restore their physical and spiritual health and life. Professional counseling can help. Exercise can also be helpful in dealing with stressors associated with a lack of motivation. Sharing personal problems with a close and trusted friend may help them think through their problems. If pastors have been overworking, perhaps a break or a vacation with the family will help. Something new and fresh to do in a different setting can bring about healing and restoration. Even Jesus needed rest from time to time. He left the crowds, the people who demanded too much from Him, and those who were plotting against Him. How much more do we as humans need to get away for a much-needed rest! When we take care of ourselves, we can then take care of others.

> God's chosen workmen should listen to the command of Christ to go apart and rest awhile. Many valuable lives have been sacrificed, that need not have been, through ignorance of this command. . . . Though the harvest is great and the laborers are few, nothing is gained by sacrificing health and life. . . . There are many feeble, worn workmen who feel deeply distressed when they see how much there is to be done, and how little they can do. How they long for physical strength to accomplish more; but it is to this class that Jesus says, "Come ye yourselves apart into a desert place, and rest awhile.[23]

Motivation is the spiritual gasoline that drives the car of ministerial success. A relentless commitment to God's will and purpose is the fuel, a never-failing strength, in pastoral life.

We need to look constantly to Jesus, realizing that it is His power which does the work. While we are to labor earnestly for the salvation of the lost, we must also take time for meditation, for prayer, and for the study of the word of God. Only the work accomplished with much prayer, and sanctified by the merit of Christ, will in the end prove to have been efficient for good.[24]

SERMON PREPARATION

On top of all the responsibilities of their vocation, pastors and other church leaders must write sermons that are original, insightful, useful, challenging, and comforting. Spiritual leaders who are committed to preaching the Word needs to spend much time studying Scripture and seeking the guidance of the Holy Spirit. The more they understand God's Word, the better they are at preparing and delivering God's message to His people. Sermon preparation usually demands more time of the pastor than any other task.

Jesus commanded the disciples, "Go into all the world and preach the gospel" (Mark 16:15). And Paul directed Timothy: "Preach the word" (2 Tim. 4:2). Preaching is the primary responsibility of the pastor. Unless he has an ardent desire in his heart, comparable to what Jeremiah felt, he cannot be an effective pastor. And Jeremiah's burden is etched to challenge preachers of all time: "His word was in mine heart as a burning fire shut up in my bones . . ." (Jer. 20:9, KJV).

Preaching is a challenging, time-consuming priority in the pastoral life. Often it takes 20 hours to prepare a Bible-based, well-constructed, spiritually effective, goal-oriented sermon. If it takes much less time than that, sermons may fall short of God's desirable goal of reaching the listeners with the convicting power of the Word. An effective sermon requires not only much study and prayer, but also a well-constructed plan of delivery and presentation. The quality of preaching should not only feed the audience with God's love, care, and expectations, but also take into account that "Christ and angels are in . . . [the] audience as listeners."[25]

There are pastors who consistently preach weak, sloppy sermons, making evident their neglect in its preparation. There are pastors who procrastinate waiting till the last minute, and working on the sermon under pressure. This is not only negligence, but also disrespect to God and His people. Every week pastors have the wonderful opportunity of presenting the Word of God. They have the spotlight precious time to inspire, teach, rebuke with grace, challenge, train, make people laugh or cry, stimulate the minds, and uphold the Savior. Pastors should not take this opportunity for granted nor fail this sacred duty of crafting a sermon worthy of the Almighty.

An effective sermon is as refreshing as the dew, as warm as rays of sunlight challenging the unknown verities of tomorrow. Researching online or repeating someone else's sermon is not the way to prepare a sermon. Only when you open God's Word to study and meditate on it, will you find the message to preach—one that will impact souls and drive them to forsake sin and surrender to Christ.

SPIRITUAL BATTLES

Looking at Peter who would play a key role in the early church, Jesus said with sadness and assurance: "Simon, Simon! Indeed, Satan has asked for you, that he may sift you as wheat. But I have prayed for you, that your faith should not fail" (Luke 22:31, 32, NKJV). Satan's masterful strategy is to discourage and derail the pastor's mission and family—such attacks weaken or bring disrepute to the mission and ministry of God's church. No wonder pastors experience an unusually high rate of stress-related illnesses, marital difficulties, conflict with their children, financial problems, and so forth.

> United with Satan in his rebellion, and with him cast out from heaven, . . . [evil spirits] have, through all succeeding ages, co-operated with him in his warfare against the divine authority. We are told in Scripture of their confederacy and government, of their various orders, of their intelligence and subtlety, and of their malicious designs against the peace and happiness of men.[26]

While such satanic scheming is not exclusive to the ministry, spiritual caregiving requires pastors, church leaders, and their families to live with extra caution and be spiritually alert. If pastors do not grow steadily toward spiritual maturity through prayer, studying God's Word, and constant fellowship with God, they may become an easy target for Satan's snares. If they do not have an abiding interest in the spiritual growth of their children, they may also be usher the children on a path away from the Lord. If they do not invest in the healthy emotional and spiritual intimacy with their spouses, both may wonder away from God in that he leaves her starving for the affection of a man while he opens himself to possible inappropriate physical intimacy elsewhere.

When a pastor is not vigilant about guarding his heart, spiritual alarms start going off. It is time to pluck out the eyes to save the soul by intentionally removing oneself from the sight of temptation. Is that painful to do when the carnal nature is strongly lured and begins to rule? Indeed! Deep hurt and fear may be felt when turning away from lust. But it has to be done and, in–Christ, can be done.

Pastor, this is crucial: Place boundaries to protect yourself and avoid ruining your life and the lives of your loved ones. As professional caregivers, pastors should know the hazards of their own fallibility.[27] Remain strong in your relationship with God. A pastor who is more focused on his own interests than God's, who neglects his personal devotions, and who trusts in his own strength and genius to the neglect of Him who enables, is a ready target for Satan's temptation.

> Satan can skillfully play the game of life with many souls, and he acts in a most underhanded, deceptive manner to spoil the faith of the people of God and to discourage them. . . . He works today as he worked in heaven, to divide the people of God in the very last stage of this earth's history. He seeks to create dissension, and to arouse contention and discussion, and to remove if possible the old landmarks of truth committed to God's people.[28]

Paul's counsel to a young pastor, Timothy, is timely: "Be strong in the grace that is in Christ Jesus" (2 Tim. 2:1). As pastors we need to remember "our strength comes from the Lord. Not from ourselves, not from anything we have achieved, not in our intellectual strength, not even in our understanding of the doctrine of Christian life and duty. All these are important, but first and foremost we must know our Lord personally, intimately, and continually."[29]

DENOMINATIONAL SUPPORT

Many pastors report that they never hear from their denominational leaders unless there is a problem or complaint. While this may be the case at times, it is good to remember that the denominational leaders' primary concern is the wellbeing of the pastor, which in turn benefits the health and growth of the church. Therefore, pastors who are going through difficulties deserve to have a safe place to turn to for help. Denominational leaders should be there to encourage pastors in their ministry, for they are the very ones who approved the pastors' ministerial credentials.

So, why are ministers not reaching out to their leaders? Some pastors fear that what they share may not be kept in confidence. Others don't want to give the impression they are doing a poor job or are discouraged. There may also be some who honestly have a fear of talking to their leaders about their professional problems and relational strains. And what if there is a sin issue? Can pastors openly speak to their superiors about it without the fear of being penalized? A healthy relationship between pastors and administrators demands close, trusting, and confiding communication.

The church is laity-oriented, but this must not be misunderstood as lack of interest in the pastorate. A healthy congregation, a caring pastor, and an involved denominational leadership are all essential for the good name and the well-being of the community of faith. Any problems, real or perceived, should be seen and resolved within this spiritual trio.

EMBRACE CHALLENGES

As fire purifies, so also difficult situations challenge us to act. Discouragement, frustrations, and misery can stimulate a desire for change and move us to focus on solutions. When we do that, problems begin to loosen their grip on our spirit; despair and uncertainty begin to fade.

When we focus on solutions, we take control. We steer our own lives, becoming the helmsman of our destiny. And we become productive because we now have a goal: exhausting all of our options to rise above the mediocre.

When our attitude is to rejoice, we can echo Paul's words spoken from a dungeon: "Rejoice in the Lord always. I will say it again: Rejoice!" (Phil. 4:4). The highs of life will bring us joy, and the lows of life will not steal the joy from us, for our eyes are set upon the Lamb of God. Thus challenging circumstances will provide us with a story to tell and empower, motivate and inspire others in ministry. By doing so, we become witnesses of God's grace, a testimony that it is possible to cope and keep moving forward even when things fall apart.

So pastor, embrace life even with all of its ups and downs. And with an attitude of gratitude, you will be able to overcome all challenges and come out of them as a conqueror.

CONCLUSION

Ministry is not defined by time, but by love. It is not governed by leadership training, but pastoral sacrifice. Its empowerment is found not in personal abilities but in God's unfailing power. Ministry is about constant relying on God and patiently working with people who are often uncommitted or infants in Christ. It is about waiting upon God while continuing to serve. Even with such apparent trials, pastoral ministry is a joy. It is the only option for the pastor or church leader who has obeyed God's calling. If you find happiness and satisfaction in something else, you are not called to be a pastor. Pastoral ministry is not an alternative or last choice for someone who has failed in every other area of life.

Pastoral ministry is serving God while expecting no greater reward than to hear those endearing words from the Lord who gave us the perfect example of ministry: "Well done, good and faithful servant!" (Matt. 25:23).

QUESTIONS FOR REFLECTION AND DISCUSSION

1. In your opinion, what is the biggest challenge in pastoral ministry? How would you deal with it?
2. Why do financial limitations affect many pastoral families in poor and rich countries?
3. In your opinion, why do some pastors and church leaders neglect their families?
4. How can a pastor or church leader overcome a lack of motivation in ministry?
5. What does it mean to have a realistic view of ministry?

ENDNOTES

[1] Ellen G. White, *Testimonies for the Church* (Mountain View, CA: Pacific Press, 1948), 1:434.

[2] White, *The Desire of Ages* (Mountain View, CA: Pacific Press, 1940), 362.

[3] Ronald V. Ash, "The Problems Facing a Pastor's Wife Today," *WLQ* 81, no. 1.

[4] White, *Gospel Workers* (Washington, DC: Review and Herald, 1915), 204.

[5] *Ibid.*

[6] Important information is available in the *Seventh-day Adventist Church Manual, Seventh-day Adventist Minister's Handbook,* and *General Conference Working Policy.*

[7] White, *The Adventist Home* (Nashville, TN: Southern Publishing, 1952), 231.

[8] Ryan Howes, *The Impact of Financial Stress,* https//www.payoff.com/life/science/impact-financial-stress/, accessed June 23, 2015.

[9] White, *The Adventist Home,* 376.

[10] *Ibid.,* 375.

[11] *Ibid.*

[12] White, *The Acts of the Apostles* (Mountain View, CA: Pacific Press, 1948), 340.

[13] *Ibid.,* 341.

14 White, *Christ's Object Lessons* (Washington, DC: Review and Herald, 1941), 342.

15 White, *Testimonies for the Church*, 9:125.

16 *Ibid.*, 8:95.

17 White, *The Great Controversy Between Christ and Satan* (Mountain View, CA: Pacific Press, 1950), 633.

18 White, *The Acts of the Apostles*, 597.

19 *Ibid.*, 50.

20 *Ibid.*, 9.

21 White, *The Desire of Ages*, 251.

22 White, *Lift Him Up* (Washington, DC: Review and Herald, 1988), 366.

23 White, *Christian Service* (Washington, DC: Review and Herald, 1947), 249.

24 White, *The Desire of Ages*, 362.

25 White, *Evangelism* (Washington, DC: Review and Herald, 1946), 184.

26 White, *The Great Controversy Between Christ and Satan*, 513.

27 Steven Foster, "Why Pastors Have Affairs: Sacred Boundaries and Sexual Abuse," FamilyFire, March 30, 2017, https://familyfire.reframemedia.com/articles/why-pastors-have-affairs, accessed September 23, 2017.

28 White, *Evangelism* (Mountain View, CA: Pacific Press, 1950), 359, 360.

29 John M. Fowler, *Ephesians: Chosen in Christ* (Hagerstown, MD: Review and Herald, 2005), 111.

CHAPTER 6

THE PASTOR'S WIFE: HER CHALLENGES

"A family that never embraces life's risks never really lives."
—Rosaria Champagne Butterfield

In today's world the role of a pastor's wife is ever changing. New opportunities open up for us to become a true helpmate to our husbands, and undertake key positions as a pastoral spouse. In addition to giving Bible studies, counseling, and partaking in other spiritual and fellowship activities, some of us even preach. And the sermons of many pastoral wives are on the same level as the best of evangelists.

Yet, in spite of all evidence that the Holy Spirit is using us women, and that God is no respecter of persons—showing no favoritism, and accepting anyone who fears Him (Acts 10:34, 35)—some church members do not welcome this contemporary role for us. They prefer that a pastoral spouse be a traditional model wife and mother, greeter, helping hand in social activities, leader in children's Sabbath School—without stepping out of the shadow of the husband. Doing so upsets some people, the intensity of which varies from congregation to congregation and culture to culture.

This set of expectations of what a pastor's wife should be, and placing limitations on what women should and should not do, can be a source of discouragement. But that need not be the case. When a pastor's wife has a realistic view of herself and, more importantly, knows what God is doing with and through her, she will develop self-confidence and a healthy self-image. She will discover that she is more than a pastor's wife, and that she is a fully-vested member in a spiritual partnership. Accepting that she is uniquely created by God for a special purpose, she will embrace whatever role God has for her. Fulfillment will replace anguish and hopelessness. She will be comfortable with who she is in God's hands, and will turn a deaf ear to criticism. She will continue to serve joyfully, following God's lead for her life in whatever role He determines for her; and will walk with assurance through any door that God opens. "When the message of God meets with opposition, He gives it additional force, that it may exert greater influence. Endowed with divine energy, it will cut its way through the strongest barrier and triumph over every obstacle."[1]

PREVALENT CHALLENGES

Among the many prevalent challenges we face as a pastoral spouse, we should not be accountable in the field of expectations. As different as people are, so also are the varied thoughts and perceptions. Every church member fosters their own unique ideas, from how a pastor and his spouse should act to what concepts and protocol should be followed in ministry. From reasonable to unreasonable, individual to collective, positive to negative, and contributory to neglectful, a world of expectations swirls around the pastor's family, and we, as pastoral wives, are no exception in taking the brunt of its verdict. What should we do? Is there a way for us to cope?

It is reasonable to expect the pastor's wife to fulfill the traditional roles of standing by her husband's side, performing peripheral church duties in support of his ministry. However, in such routines, it is possible to make room for individuality and variety, according to her personality, which makes for a unique contribution to congregational life. But her greatest ongoing battle is balancing the conflict between the expectations of others and her desire to be true to herself, especially when God is prompting her to step up her involvement in ministry. Thankfully, through God, a pastoral wife can retain her uniqueness, regardless of her disturbing surroundings and the expectations of her. As God's children, "we have an individuality and an identity that is our own. No one can submerge his identity in that of any other. All must act for themselves, according to the dictates of their own conscience."[2] Indeed, this is the case of a pastoral spouse, and I, Raquel, will discuss five important expectations women face:

1. The church organization's expectations. Feeling unsure about being a pastor's wife is a big challenge in itself. Pastors receive training for their job and how they should relate to the conference, but the pastoral spouse does not. Yet some local conferences or missions expect pastoral spouses to be facilitators of communication between the organization and the pastor or congregation, as may be needed. And they further suppose that it is her duty to be involved in different aspects of ministry as a volunteer.

In this difficult area, as pastoral spouses, we need to understand how the church organization, such as a conference/union/division/General Conference, functions: What is the mission of the local conference? What is its organizational structure? How do the various levels of the church organization interact with each other? Who are the officers and departmental directors? What functions do they perform? And, lastly, how do these functions relate to the local church? Considering these intricacies, organizational leaders should periodically conduct seminars that facilitate spouses' understanding of the organizational structure of the church.

2. The congregation's expectations. The expectations of the local church are quite high for the pastor's spouse and family. Church members expect pastoral spouses to be involved in almost everything: music, Bible studies, women's or children's ministries, hospitality, outreach, etc. They are also expected to show up for baby showers, bridal showers, weddings, funerals, and more. The list is endless. To expect pastoral spouses to assume all these responsibilities is burdensome, unrealistic, and unreasonable.

Here's where the church nominating committee can creatively exercise its leadership. First, the committee should recognize the unreasonable expectations of the pastoral spouse. Second, they should work in close consultation with the spouse to understand her talents and the time she has to give, making sure she is not overburdened or monopolized in one area of church life. Third, the committee should identify people in the congregation who could pool their talents to serve the various needs of the church.

By meeting the expectations of the congregation this way, the nominating committee gives a signal to the congregation that, while the pastoral couple are there to serve the congregation, they are not to be overwhelmed with duties to the point of being victims of burnout. Supporting them empowers them to be fountains of blessings to the entire congregation.

3. The spouse's expectations. Ask any man—even more so, ask any pastor—what he hopes to see in his wife, and, without skipping a beat, his answer would be close to Proverbs 31: a wife who is "of noble character" (v. 10); gains her husband's "full confidence" (v. 11); "brings him good, not harm, all the days of her life" (v. 12); is industrious, manages her home well, cares for and builds her community (vv. 12–19); "opens her arms to the poor and extends her hands to the needy" (v. 20); manages her household well (vv. 21, 22); "is clothed with strength and dignity," "speaks with wisdom," and "watches over the affairs of her household" (vv. 25–27); and "fears the Lord" (v. 30).

Such expectations may be high, and correspondingly similar to the expectations his wife has of him. Their hopes are reciprocal and certainly within the biblical concept of marriage: the two "become one flesh" (Gen. 2:23, 24). Within their sacred unity, a pastoral couple should be deeply involved in their interpersonal calling—exhibiting love, affection, care, concern, loyalty, faith, trust, and mutual confidence; being involved in family worship, child-care, and growth; contributing to community building; and so forth.

Pastors, encourage your spouses to serve the church as the Lord leads them. Help them find roles in the church that use their spiritual gifts/talents and bring them joy. If there are some who think the church should get two for the price of one, make it clear, kindly and with tact, that pastoral spouses are not a commodity. They are not multifunctional instruments to be utilized in different aspects of ministry as members see fit. Like everyone else, they have limited time and prior commitments to God, their spouses and children. They she should have the freedom to offer their talents to the ministry of the church with joy.

4. Self-expectations. While the pastoral spouses may want to meet different expectations, they must not neglect their own self-expectations. Unless they have well-defined goals, they will not reach their full potential. They may want to use their gifts to enhance God's kingdom and meet the varied demands of them as pastoral spouses, but to attain this objective, they should seek opportunities to expand their mental, social, spiritual, and educational horizons. This will increase their service potential even as their spouses' ministries grow.

Sometimes pastoral spouses may think they should be in the back-ground. After all, besides fulfilling traditional ministerial duties, they have to care for their children and households. True enough, but God expects all of us to keep growing in the talents and professional interests entrusted to us. Pastoral spouses should develop whatever professional talents and gifts they have.

> Many who are qualified to do excellent work accomplish little be-cause they attempt little. Thousands pass through life as if they had no great object for which to live, no high standard to reach. One reason for this is the low estimate which they place upon themselves. Christ paid an infinite price for us, and according to the price paid He desires us to value ourselves.[3]

What should pastoral spouses do to increase their self-expectations? Begin with a thorough and honest self-examination. Ask yourself: What do I love to do? When given a list of activities to accomplish, what do I first grav-itate toward? What do I love to do for a period of time? What is the most fulfilling ministry-related activity I would like to do? What activity that I have undertaken in the past has been the most fulfilling? Most likely, some activities will inherently be more comfortable and rewarding than others. In these areas, others may admire you and, yet, you may not feel you are doing anything challenging or particularly special.

Finally, as a pastoral spouse, keep a prayer in your heart throughout the day, saying: Father, draw me close to You, for I seek to know You. Give me wisdom to interact with my spouse, children, and church family, that I may be cordial, polite, patient, and compassionate. May I not cause them any sorrow in word or deed, for I long to be Your daughter. Teach me how to train my children that they will bring honor and glory to You. I want to be tenderhearted and forgiving toward my spouse, never taking offense by misinterpreting words and motives. Mold me into Your character of love. I love you, Lord. Thank you for the Holy Spirit. Thank you for Jesus. In His name I pray, Amen.

5. God's expectations. God's promise for all His children, including those married to pastors, is "Do not fear, for I have redeemed you; I have summoned you by name; you are mine" (Isa. 43:1). Thus you fulfill the most important expectation God has in you: you are His child, witness, and messenger in your church and community. To fulfill such an expectation from God is neither easy nor something to be taken lightly. God has called you to bear His name, be His witness, stand at the right hand of your spouse, and reach the ideal God expects from you.

Therefore, as a pastoral spouse, "consecrate yourself to God in the morning; make this your very first work. Let your prayer be, 'Take me, O Lord, as wholly Thine. I lay all my plans at Thy feet. Use me today in Thy service. Abide with me, and let all my work be wrought in Thee.' . . . Each morning consecrate yourself to God for that day. Surrender all your plans to Him, to be carried out or given up as His providence shall indicate. Thus day by day you may be giving your life into the hands of God, and thus your life will be molded more and more after the life of Christ."[4]

CRITICISM

As long as there is community life and interaction with people, a pastoral spouse will have to expect both appreciation and criticism. We counsel you to accept appreciation with humility, and bear criticism with grace. In the long run, learning to deal with criticism can be an effective instrument of spiritual growth and character development.

Regardless of the criticism and of whom it concerns—you, your spouse, your children, or even a friend—it is deeply hurtful. People can be very cruel. If you are criticized to your face, reply politely, with kindness and grace, "You don't know all of the facts; excuse me," and then walk away. Most people will think twice before criticizing you again. There is no need to explain yourself to them because your words may only add to their fuel of misinterpretation.

But if someone criticizes others to you, an appropriate response may be, "Why don't we both talk to that person and counsel them about it, or would you prefer that I talk to them first and then ask them to speak to you?" it's important to let them know that the person they are criticizing will find out about their meddling, and would probably rather not be in the spotlight. Of course, if the criticizing is petty, do not follow through; instead drop the matter because you do not want to fuel animosity between brethren. But if the ministry of that other person is at risk, you may need to pray and follow through. Regardless, your response should stop complainers in their tracks.

What if criticism is done behind your back and you come to find out about it? Weigh the issue. Is it worth making a big deal about it? Or, should you ignore it? No matter what the criticism is, it is necessary to share grace and exercise forgiveness. Wounded persons can easily become bitter. If your defense is to pray for your critics, you will find that you cannot stay angry with those for whom you are praying. Along with prayer, relate to them in love (Matt. 5:39), choose not to dwell on your wounded spirit (Phil. 4:8), learn to forgive (Matt. 6:5–15), and extend to them the same undeserved love that Christ has shown you (Rom. 3:10–12, 23, 24). Remember, Christian love is not just about loving the lovable, but also loving those who hurt, hate, and humiliate. Charles Swindoll, well-known author and pastor, once said, "Life is 10 percent what happens to you and 90 percent how you react to it."[5]

Associating with all church members peacefully and lovingly can be a challenge, but the Christian calling demands of us to live in peace with one another. Paul counsels, "If it is possible, as far as it depends on you, live at peace with everyone" (Rom. 12:18). Paul concedes that peace is not always possible. However, take responsibility for the part over which you have control. Make your priorities obvious. Let the congregation know what's important to you. Do not allow others to squeeze you into their mold. Live in love, seek grace at all times, and pray for peace that only the Holy Spirit can give.

MARRIAGE AND FAMILY
Every marriage has its challenges, even under the best of circumstances. But the marriage of a pastoral couple undergoes additional challenges that threaten the quality of the couples relationship and the success of their joint ministry. Here are some of those challenges:

Time management. It seems like there is never enough time to meet all the demands of the day. Relationships, especially that of pastoral couples, are threatened without quality time. Both the husband and wife need to balance their time in such a way that their precious relationship is not affected or neglected.

> God wants the home to be the happiest place on earth, the very symbol of the home in heaven. Bearing the marriage responsibilities in the home, linking their interests with Jesus Christ, leaning upon His arm and His assurance, husband and wife may share a happiness in this union that angels of God commend.[6]

Closeness. Maintaining the closeness of marriage is in itself a challenge for the pastoral couple. It may sound strange, but it needs to be said that a pastoral marriage is public. The pastoral couple's interactions are watched, scrutinized, critiqued, criticized, and, if good, they inspire others. Pastors often preach on marriage and offer from the pulpit sound advice on maintaining stability and happiness in married life. Even as pastors preach about this, the congregation critiques the sermon. Therefore, pastors should strive to practice what they preach.

Reciprocal values. Another significant challenge in pastoral marriages is ensuring that both husband and wife have and practice the basic ingredients of a happy relationship: unconditional love, positive mutual regard, open communication, trust in each other, and unwavering commitment. When these ingredients exist in a marriage, the couple enjoy a relationship that flourishes in mutual love, goodwill, forbearance, and a readiness to overcome obstacles. A successful marriage may have problems, but the husband and wife navigate the family as a pastoral team with the Lord whom serves as their chief pilot in their lives, ministry, and home.

Keeping alive the magic of love. Everything in life requires maintenance, including love in a marriage. A pastor cannot use the excuse of being busy in God's work to neglect the details and romance that makes for a happy marriage. Authentic interaction with each other, holding hands and laughing while chatting, leisurely sharing anecdotes and reminiscing, and sharing their feelings and ideas, all work together to open their hearts to each other and strengthen the foundation of their love.

> Your companionship in the marriage relation should be close and tender, holy and elevated, breathing a spiritual power into your

lives, that you may be everything to each other that God's word requires. When you reach the condition that the Lord desires you to reach, you will find heaven below and God in your life.[7]

LONELINESS

Ministry demands that pastors spend a lot of time outside of the home with people—visiting, studying, praying, counseling, preparing for baptism, chairing boards, etc. Yet the most common concern of pastoral spouses is loneliness, resulting from being married to pastors who do not have time to spend with them. Some church members assume that, since the pastoral couple spends a lot of time together, they are strong enough to handle any problem. Wrong. A pastor may live in the same house as his wife, but if they take no time to share their lives, to seek God's help to resolve their mutual problems, and share their joy, loneliness can erode their union spiritually and otherwise.

A house with love in it, where love is expressed in words and looks and deeds, is a place where angels love to manifest their presence and hallow the scene by rays of light from glory. There the humble household duties have a charm in them. None of life's duties will be unpleasant to your wife under such circumstances. She will perform them with cheerfulness of spirit and will be like a sunbeam to all around her, and she will be making melody in her heart to the Lord.[8]

Jesus is the ultimate answer to loneliness. In His presence, the potential to grow closer and more intimate is limitless. He is the definitive place of rest, healing, wholeness, perspective, and comfort. He is the one support system that is instant, constant, and consistent. Invest heavily in Him, and His presence in your heart will be a balm for your soul.

DEPRESSION

It is a fact that pastoral spouses face depression. Ministry, by its very nature, is a relational profession where pastors and their spouses constantly relate to individuals with varied stresses and emotional problems. While pastoral couples attend to them, their contact should be limited to prayer, spiritual encouragement, and emotional comfort. They should not go into areas that are best handled by trained mental health professionals. At the same time, if pastors or their spouses experience symptoms of depression, they must seek professional assistance. Remember, getting help is nothing to be ashamed of. Instead, seeking help at an early stage can prevent a long-term emotional illness.

Depression in any member of the pastoral family should not be ignored. The whole family needs to show concern, offer understanding, and, above all, pray and support the individual. Both in its effects and in its cry for help, depression is a family matter. The issue should be discussed as a family, and the solutions should be approached as a family.

When pastors become the unfortunate victims of depression, they can lean not only on the love and support of their spouses and families, but also on their larger family of church leadership, who could be helpful in arranging for professional assistance. They could also help or rearrange family priorities and professional responsibilities. In most cases depression is a temporary state of mind and can be treated from both a spiritual and a psychological perspective.

No assistance is as effective in dealing with the beginnings of depression as building a home and church fellowship that share, openly and without hesitation the bonds of love, mutual respect and honor, an attitude of care and concern, and a fostering of a close-knit family tie. Where these qualities of a godly family and fellowship are absent, there is a danger of division and disillusionment. "Angels flee from the dwelling where words of discord are exchanged, where gratitude is almost a stranger to the heart, and censure leaps like black balls to the lips, spotting the garments, defiling the Christian character."[9]

Let me share a personal experience. Years ago, depression hit me—not very hard, but real nevertheless. I don't know what triggered it or why it had a hold on me, but I do know the experience was real and the recovery was a miracle brought about by my heavenly Father. During the deepest periods of my depression, I found no joy or meaning in life. No activity brought me out of the darkness. I lacked motivation and no accomplishments gave me satisfaction. I was no longer interested in anything. The limit of my daily activities was to wake up in the morning, brush my teeth, get dressed, take care of my children, wave goodbye to Jonas, and get back into bed. I was aboard the speeding train of depression.

But, thank God, the train didn't crashed. I found help. It came from many sources. My family, particularly my husband, stood by me. They gave me unreserved love, understanding, and support. Family, by the very definition, should uplift, and that is what they did. When even the daily routines seemed burdensome and overwhelming, Jonas, with a willing spirit, took it upon himself to help me.

Depression is a serious disease, and it is important that we seek help as soon as possible. Do not wait, and do not keep it a secret. Depression is a problem that can be treated, but not by yourself. Get the help you need. Talk to your spouse. He is the person who should help you feel most secure. Confide in him. Pray with him. Live closely with God, and draw strength from Him. God never allows anything in our lives that we cannot handle with His help. Make the psalmist's prayer your own: "Why, my soul, are you downcast? Why so disturbed within me? Put your hope in God" (Ps. 43:5).

I find much strength in the Psalms. David often experienced rejection and depression in his life. Even his family and those he trusted most injured his soul and swayed his confidence. But during moments of depression, he found his peace and solace in God:

> Even though I walk
> through the darkest valley,
> I will fear no evil,
> for you are with me;
> your rod and your staff,
> they comfort me. (Ps. 23:4)

The God who was with David, Moses, Elijah, Daniel, Esther, and Paul, is the same One with me. It is that confidence and strength that enabled me to overcome my moments of depression and battle with the enemy. And God can be your help too. God knows what we go through. He is aware of our struggles. Then, when we come out on the other side, we can praise Him and give Him the glory!

AUTHENTICITY

Authenticity can be a challenge for a pastoral spouse. The apostle Paul never doubted his mission or his calling. "By the grace of God I am what I am" (1 Cor. 15:10). Likewise, pastoral spouses must find authenticity not in being married to a pastor, but in Whom they serve. God's grace called you and enabled you to be a pastoral spouse. In Him you will find inner strength and outer protection to accomplish your mission as your spouse's helpmate in ministry. In God's work, there is no room for self-authentication. It is the Holy Spirit that leads in ministry those who undergo the experience of Paul: "I have been crucified with Christ and I no longer live, but Christ lives in me. The life I now live in the body, I live by faith in the Son of God, who loved me and gave himself for me" (Gal. 2:20).

If you have identified fully with Jesus, you are free to be yourself. Your eyes will manifest peace. Your face will reflect joy. Your appearance will be relaxed because you do not carry the burden of not being your authentic self. And your contentment will be contagious. You will be ready to minister anywhere in the church, and your natural glow of authenticity will be a welcomed breath of fresh air for parishioners.

But, if on a given day you are tired, a little under the weather, or even sad, don't wear a mask and pretend you are okay because you are your authentic self all of the time. Your church family will see an authentic human being who has ups and downs like everybody else. And your transparency will open doors for them to reach out to you with their joys and challenges. It is the door of friendship that you will have unlocked by being your authentic self in Christ.

PASTORAL MOVES

A new chapter opens for the pastoral family. Somewhere on the horizon God has a place for them. In some areas, pastoral moves occur every two to four years. This is particularly stressful to the spouse, especially when the couple has children. Yet the time comes to say goodbye to their current church family. A new beginning awaits.

New assignments are frequently offered to or pursued by a pastor. With much consideration and prayer, a determination is made. The pastor's expertise and energy are just what is needed in another church many miles away, and both the family and the conference under which they labor are convicted that God approves of the move.

But at times, when pastors announce from the pulpit that they will soon bid farewell, some of those who criticized the pastoral family, suddenly feel the move is unfair. It is good to have a change of heart, repent, and mend our ways; it is godly to do so. Some may apologize verbally. Others in deeds by showing kindness at the last minute. A pastoral family should walk out of the old church with dignity, not holding grudges, but convinced that the Holy Spirit is actively working in the hearts of everyone.

Yet, all is not sadness. Old friendships can continue across the miles, especially in the present age where technology makes it very easy to do so. Embracing new friends offers unique blessings, opportunities to learn and share, new experiences in camaraderie, and wonderful adventures in building memories. By expanding our sphere of influence, new friendships can be a mutual blessing. This agrees with the prayer of Jabez—"Oh, that you would bless me and enlarge my territory!" (1 Chron. 4:10), and God answered Jabez's cry. Such also is what Isaiah describes:

> Enlarge the place of your tent,
> And let them stretch out the curtains of your dwellings;
> Do not spare;
> Lengthen your cords,
> And strengthen your stakes. (54:2, NKJV)

Fresh new opportunities for change stimulates church growth, and the pastoral family can further develop their talents. Many throughout the Bible were summoned to a new destiny: Jonah goes to Nineveh, Ezekiel to Babylon, Esther finds her place in Shushan, Philip catches up to a chariot on the Gaza road, Peter goes to Cornelius, Barnabas to Antioch, Paul to Macedonia, and John goes to Patmos.

The gospel mission has always been on the move, from Jerusalem to the ends of the earth. The pastoral family should be ready to move whenever the time appointed by God is come, and wherever the Holy Spirit leads them. So must also their current church—while it has been blessed by their ministry, it's time to wave goodbye and wish them well: "Keep in touch. Be safe. Godspeed!"

THE SABBATHS

The Bible describes the Sabbath as "a delight" and "honorable" (see Isa. 58:13). How could it then be a challenge to the pastoral spouses? When Sabbath hours draw near, all secular work needs to be completed: cleaning the house; preparing food for Sabbath; getting the clothes ready; and other personal details. In a pastor's home, most of this work on preparation day falls on the shoulders of the spouse, especially when the children are young.

Then, on Sabbath morning, there are more responsibilities: breakfast, morning worship, dressing younger children, sending off the pastor for an early service or a different church. Then it is that spouse who takes the children to church.

At the church, there are even more responsibilities—in Sabbath School, worship or fellowship. There is also the interacts with people, including those who complain, criticize, or meddle. Of course, there are also the opportunity to refresh the spirit chatting with those who are true friends, and thankful for the pastoral spouse's involvement in ministry.

Now it is Sabbath afternoon. The church has several activities planned, and the pastor as couple are sometimes expected to attend. The Sabbath, which is meant to be a delight and a blessing, may often end up being the most stressful day of the week. What could be done to make the Sabbath what is meant to be, a day for physical rest, when the mind puts worries on hold, a delight for the spirit, and the heart that is one with God? Here are a few suggestions for the very busy pastoral spouse:

Prepare a list of all that needs to be accomplished before the Sabbath, and do a little bit every day, so on Friday, before the hours of the Sabbath begin, all you have to do is touch up again and cook. Each detail you accomplish throughout the week is a refreshing anticipation of the delight you will experience on the Sabbath, God's holy day. To those who are committed to His holiness, God will not make that day a burdensome one. To them it will indeed be a day of joy and blessings.

PASTOR'S SPOUSE AND WOMEN'S MINISTRY

Should a pastor's spouse be expected to always serve as the leader of women's ministries in the church? Just because the prior pastoral spouse served as such, is it reasonable to assume that the new pastor and his wife should also be the leader of women's ministries? The expectation itself is not biblical. Paul lists the spiritual gifts as follows: "There are diversities of gifts, but the same Spirit. There are differences of ministries, but the same Lord. And there are diversities of activities, but it is the same God who works all in all" (1 Cor. 12:4–6, NKJV).

Each woman differs in the ministry according to the gifts God has bestowed upon her. Some are gifted in Sabbath School ministry, some in children's ministry, some in Pathfinders, some in community service, some in prayer ministry, some in personal evangelism, and some in women's ministries. It is not fair for a congregation to expect that a pastor's wife be involved in a particular ministry without giving her a choice. The pastoral spouse must have the same freedom, as anyone else does, to choose her ministry, taking into account her talents, calling, and other responsibilities she may already have. It is possible that while she may not wish to serve in a primary role as a women's ministry director, she may volunteer to be of assistance whenever called upon. The main point is, she should not be deprived of the freedom to serve the church using the gifts that the Spirit has given to her.

"I WISH I HAD KNOWN THAT!"

"I wish someone had told me what to expect as a pastor's spouse!" We all wish we had some secret code or device that alerts us of the pains and possibilities, the hows and how–not–tos, and the dos and don'ts of life. But our life road map is not made up of such wishes. Nevertheless, we cannot dismiss our desires altogether.

What do you wish you had been told before you became a minister's spouse? Consider the following from a list of wishes that a contemporary Christian author compiled:[10]

1. **I wish someone had told me just to be myself.** "I am a people-pleaser by nature, so for me, not being prepared to handle being a pastor's wife with my personality was a heavy burden to carry early in our ministry."

2. **I wish someone had prepared me to deal with criticism of my husband and me.** "It was hard to deal with negative experiences, conflicts, or criticisms, especially in relation to my husband and our area of ministry. So I would harbor feelings of resentment when it came to ministry and my man."

3. **I wish someone had told me that others were always watching us.** "Even though they are watching us, we don't need to be controlled by what they expect of us."

4. **I wish someone had told me how much my husband needs me to build him up.** "I need to be his cheerleader. Dealing with critics in the church is difficult. He needs to hear that I respect him now more than ever."

5. **I wish someone had told me that my schedule would never be normal again.** "Your husband will be very busy. Expect that. But come alongside him in the areas of time management and organization."

As the wife of a pastor, I wish to give you a head start. Be yourself. Be prepared to deal with criticism about you and your husband. You are being watched. Your husband needs your support and encouragement. Be ready to reschedule your well-planned life, and then to reschedule it again. If you understand this and are ready, and willing to front the storms ahead, you will enjoy being a pastoral spouse.

CONCLUSION

Pastoral wives were asked a question for a research project: "If you had a chance to live your life over, would you still want to be a pastor's wife?" The answer was astounding. Almost every one of them said, "Yes, absolutely!" To the researcher that meant they said "it has been worth it—all the good times and all the hard times."[11]

"Who can represent the truth and the example of Christ better than Christian women who themselves are practicing the truth?"[12] Pastoral spouses who have dedicated their lives to stand by their husbands in serving Jesus and ministering to His people need to develop a personal vision and spiritual perspective that will help them succeed in their team ministry. The following would help in their role as pastoral spouses:[13]

- See the big picture. This ministry is not about you! It's about transforming people's lives. Watch and see how God does great things in simple lives!
- Learn how to be flexible. Each day will come with new challenges. Approach each day as an adventure, and seek God's assistance afresh.
- Don't take things personally. Accept joys and disappointments as they come your way in your daily interactions with people. Remember, "all things work together for good to those who love God, to those who are the called according to His purpose" (Rom. 8:28, NKJV).
- Be secure and content with yourself. Each person has a different personality and way of looking at things. Do not try to be what you think others want you to be.
- Be yourself and be true to who you are! This will come when you are assured of your position in Christ. Knowing Whose you are will give you the confidence to be who God created you to be.
- And most important of all, have a relationship with the Lord that encompasses every area of your life!

As a pastoral spouse, you will find the following promise, given to women in general, reassuring when facing challenges in life:

> Great is the work and mission of women. . . . They can be a blessing to all around them. They can have a powerful influence for good if they will let their light so shine that others may be led to glorify our heavenly Father. Women may have a transforming influence if they will only consent to yield their way and their will to God, and let Him control their mind, affections, and being. They can have an influence which will tend to refine and elevate those with whom they associate. . . . [In them] self is forgotten, merged in the life of Christ. To be rich in good works is as natural as their breath. They live to do others good.[14]

QUESTIONS FOR REFLECTION OR DISCUSSION

1. Can you recall some of the blessings and burdens of being a pastor's spouse? Which one would you say is the greatest blessing, and which is the heaviest burden?
2. Where do your spouse and you find your own pastoral care?
3. How do you deal with criticism from your church members?
4. What is important to know before deciding to become a pastor's spouse?
5. If you had a chance to live your life over again, would you still want to be a pastor's spouse?

ENDNOTES

[1] Ellen G. White, *The Acts of the Apostles* (Mountain View, CA: Pacific Press, 1911), 601.

[2] White, *Testimonies to Ministers and Gospel Workers* (Mountain View, CA: Pacific Press, 1944), 422.

[3] White, *Gospel Workers* (Washington, DC: Review and Herald, 1915), 291.

[4] White, *Steps to Christ* (Washington, DC: Review and Herald, 1956), 70.

[5] Adapted from Stacey Weeks, "Not Just One of the Girls," *Just Between Us*, http://justbetweenus.org/ministry/pastors-wives/pastors-wives-finding-contentment/, accessed July 15, 2016.

[6] White, *The Adventist Home* (Nashville, TN: Southern Publishing, 1952), 102.

[7] *Ibid.*, 112.

[8] *Ibid.*, 109.

[9] White, *Testimonies for the Church* (Mountain View, CA: Pacific Press, 1948), 1:696.

[10] Adapted from Thom S. Rainer. "Seven Things Pastors' Wives Wish They Had Been Told Before They Became Pastors' Wives," April 6, 2013, http://thomrainer.com/2013/04/seven-things-pastors-wives-wish-they-had-been-told-before-they-became-pastors-wives/, accessed July 15, 2016.

[11] See Benoit, "Changing Role of the Pastor's Wife," 101, 114.

[12] White, *Evangelism* (Washington, DC: Review and Herald, 1946), 467.

[13] Adapted from Benoit, "Changing Role of the Pastor's Wife," 102.

[14] White, *Testimonies for the Church*, 2:465.

CHAPTER 7

MARRIAGE AND FAMILY

"You don't choose your family. They are God's gift to you, as you are to them."—Desmond Tutu

Everyone wants to have a happy marriage. Those of us who answered God's calling to be pastors are no exception. Indeed, a joyful pastoral family can be a model to their church family, inspiring married folks to also yearn for a loving, blessed relationship. For the pastoral couple, the bond of a healthy and happy marriage strengthens their union and is a witness and asset to their ministry.

Although a pastor and spouse will never be perfect, they can still be prepared to meet specific challenges that may threaten to affect their marriage, family life, and ministry. In this chapter we discuss six practical and essential principles to help you build an exemplary and uplifting model for your pastoral family: (1) Your family is your first ministry; (2) Nurture your marriage; (3) Care for your children; (4) Live life together; (5) Relate well to your spouse; and (6) Be balanced. Let us begin!

YOUR FAMILY IS YOUR FIRST MINISTRY

We are to bloom where we are planted, and our home and family is where our ministry should bloom first. Pastors have answered the call to minister God's people, but love begins at home. When I started my ministry, I was made aware of a very sensible warning: "Do not sacrifice your family on the altar of ministry." I invite all pastors to consider that wise counsel and live up to it.

But ministry can become addictive. Pastors are often misled into thinking they can solve every problem in the world, yet that is a great deception. If pastors prioritize ministering to others, they will create a problem in their own lives by neglecting their family and weakening relationships with their loved ones. Due to their neglect of their spousal and parental pledge, some pastors have lost their families. Pastors' commitments must be balanced between their hard work in ministry and caring for their families. But family is priority. Our spouses did not marry the church; they married us! Hence, we need to commit to making our marriages work. And it is worth it!

Pastors are blessed with flexible schedules so that, without neglecting their ministerial work, they can dedicate quality time at home. Most people in other lines of work cannot do that. But a pastor's schedule can be adjusted on occasion to have lunch at home with the family, attend school functions, etc. Pastors can make the best of their daily routines with those blessings that flexibility offers. Pastor, be conscious of your commitment as a spouse and parent. Love your nest. Guard your nest. Your family is your first ministry.

NURTURING YOUR MARRIAGE

Those who neglect their spouse quickly learn how unfruitful their ministry to the church becomes. The ministry of service in the home develops the healthy foundation that then spills out and blesses the children placed in the care of the pastoral couple.

Therefore, learn how to nurture and protect your marital relationship. Every day, give it the time and effort necessary for it to grow and become closer in love, stronger in affection, and caring in all things. There will be times when you and your spouse disagree on certain issues, and that is the time both of you need to learn how to guard and take care of your marriage. The divine prescription that in marriage "the two become one flesh" emphasizes the priority of oneness and unity—in body, mind, and spirit—that should govern the relationship between husband and wife. That means the two of you must learn to communicate with each other as best of friends with the best of interests for both.

Remember: never fight with each other, but rather fight for each other, build each other up, develop trust in each other, serve each other, rejoice in each other, keep no secrets from one another, and build a home where love and trust abound. Safeguard your union and home for your sake and for the sake of your children. Create a dwelling that gives them the blessing of living in a home that offers fairness and understanding, safety and protection, rest and peace.

When I began my ministry, within my heart there was a passion to make a difference. Such an urge is normal and proper. Were it not for that urge, being in the ministry would not have been meaningful. That is because ministry can be burdensome—it does not bring continuous joy. But young pastors may be so consumed by ministry that they neglect their families. It may not be intentional, but the result is the same. If not vigilant, they will drive themselves out of their own family lives. Their spouses and children will taste what it is like to be a widow/widower and orphans because, though their bodies show up at home, their minds and spirits are not engaged in the family unit.

Nothing is more important to me as a pastor than my relationship with Jesus and my relationship with my wife and family. Even here I need to make a distinction: my relationship with Jesus and my relationship to ministry are two different matters; they are at either end of my relationship with my wife and family. To me, Jesus is priority, then comes my wife and family, then my ministry. Jesus is in favor of my being successful in all of life's endeavors. He guides and gives me wisdom to accomplish His vision that my homelife be a haven and witness to my mission. So let all pastors care for their own first. Ministry is demanding, but it will always be there. Give yourself permission to spend time and have fun with your spouse. You will be much more effective if your house is in order than if you neglect the covenant you entered into with your spouse.

If a pastoral couple is to be successful in ministry as a team, they need to set boundaries from the beginning—boundaries for their marriage, family, and ministry. When they discuss these boundaries and put them into place, they should work as a couple within those boundaries.

> God wants the home to be the happiest place on earth, the very symbol of the home in heaven. Bearing the marriage responsibilities in the home, linking their interests with Jesus Christ, leaning upon His arm and His assurance, husband and wife may share a happiness in this union that angels of God commend.[1]

To be a blessing in your ministerial work, learn to love your spouse better, stronger, and more faithfully every day. Make your goal this daily nurturing commitment. Marriage was instituted in Eden; the church came later on. You can accomplish great things in ministry if you have a supportive spouse by your side, but you must be your spouse's support also. There is an African proverb that says, "If you want to go fast, go alone. But if you want to go far, go together." The life and health of the church reflects the life and health of the pastoral couple. Do not put in jeopardy your church ministry because you try to go fast by doing too much yourself, because you may end up alone with a failed marriage. In ministry, you want the gospel to reach the ends of the world, as commissioned by Christ. Therefore, go together, and you will be a blessing to your spouse and a blessing to your church.

CARE FOR YOUR CHILDREN

Being a pastor's child is unique and makes for an interesting journey. The Lord is your greatest help in nurturing children to grow to love and serve Him.

> The Christian's first duty is in the home. Fathers and mothers, yours is a great responsibility. You are preparing your children for life or for death; you are training them for an abiding place here in the earth, for self-gratification in this life, or for the immortal life, to praise God forever. And which shall it be? It should be the burden of your life to have every child that God has committed to your trust receive the divine mold.[2]

The above quote addresses fathers and mothers alike. But it often seems that in the case where one parent is also a pastor, the pastor parent spends far less time than the other in childcare, nurture, and development. The pastor parent is often busy, particularly in the evenings when the children are home. There may be committee meetings, home visits, Bible studies, and many other ministry obligations.

A pastor who fails to schedule specific periods of time to be home and tend to the family will miss out on the most important responsibility entrusted to parents: raising children to be strong, mature, and responsible for God's kingdom. Placing the burden of child rearing solely on the spouse can put her or him at risk of becoming frustrated, irritated, and resentful. Their marriage will be thus negatively affected by the pastor's absenteeism. And the spouse's hurting spirit speaks volumes about the pastor's neglect of family duties.

What, then, is the responsibility of pastors with respect to their role as parents?

1. Make the home the first priority of the pastor's work. Both the pastor and the spouse should have a joint understanding and mutual appreciation of their role in childcare and development. A pastor should have his or her calendar arranged to spend sufficient time with the entire family, so that children get from both parents the needed love and care, discipline and nurture, spiritual growth and social stability. "Give your children intellectual culture and moral training. Fortify their young minds with firm, pure principles. While you have opportunity, lay the foundation for a noble manhood and womanhood. Your labor will be rewarded a thousandfold."[3]

2. Have your church understand the role of the pastor's family in the life of the church and the congregation. The pastor is the minister

of the church, with responsibilities to the congregation. While the pastor's spouse may play a special role in the life of the church (as discussed in an earlier chapter), it is not fair to expect the pastor's children to be equally involved. They should not be made to act any different than other children in the church. Hopefully they set a positive and exemplary lifestyle because of their own walk with the Lord, and not just because their parent is a pastor. They deserve a life as normal as the lives of other children; they should neither think they are missing out on something, nor feel they are more special than others.

3. Make sure the conversations you have with your spouse are wholesome, not negative and critical. Do not discuss problems within the church in front of your children. Ensure they do not become bitter and angry if they happen to see or hear negative things from or about church members. There may be times when conflicts within the church, between the pastor and some members of the congregation, have a negative impact on the children. They will feel caught in the middle, and often feel rejected by their own friends. At such times, keep your communication lines open between you and your children. Always be available to listen to and pray with them.

4. Remember your children are always your children—in good times and hard times, in times of success and times of failure, in situations when they make you proud and incidents when you feel let down. Your love and affection for them, and your care and prayers for them, must not be dictated or distracted by others. Love them unconditionally at all times, and pray for them continually. No matter how old your children are, they will always be your children, even though the nature of the relationship will change. Nurture your relationship with them early in life so that when they get older you will have not only a wonderful child, but also a wonderful friend!

A pastor committed as a parent helps advance children's Christian values and maturity by showing deeply committed love and affection for their mother. The pastoral couple are to be a role model for their children. In turn, the pastoral family will be a role model for not only their church, but also their community. With such a witness in their midst, the congregation readily gives the pastoral family the room and support they need to grow so that they as a whole may be "built together to become a dwelling in which God lives by his Spirit" (Eph. 2:22).

LIVE LIFE TOGETHER

"Togetherness" is the key word for the pastoral family. Remember, it all began because God made a man and a woman to be together. He so determined it since creation week that both of you should become one (Gen. 2:24), to honor each other (Eph. 5:22–33), love each other (Eph. 5:25), and remain together until death separates you (Matt. 19:9). He united the two of you for a reason, not by accident, and you have now grown into a family with children of your own. The concept of togetherness, based on genuine love for each other, is the glue that keeps the husband and wife bonded as one in body and spirit.

Because of this, togetherness is one of the key ingredients that make up not only a successful marriage, but also a loving family. As a result, a couple can positively affirm, "We are in this together and are stronger. The tie that binds us can never be broken." Consider again these words:

God wants the home to be the happiest place on earth, the very symbol of the home in heaven. Bearing the marriage responsibilities in the home, linking their interests with Jesus Christ, leaning upon His arm and His assurance, husband and wife may share a happiness in this union that angels of God commend.[4]

Why is togetherness so important for marital health? Why is it necessary for families to spend time together? Like most others, I, too, feel there are just not enough hours in a day to spend with my family. Meanwhile, I have often wondered which is better for family togetherness, quality time or quantity time?

More recent research shows that kids need *both* with their parents. In fact, the more involved parents are with their children—and the word "more" here is used with direct reference to the concept of quantity—the less likely they are to have social, emotional, or academic problems, use drugs or alcohol, become involved in crime, or engage in premarital sex.[5]

Hence quality time emerges from quantity time: the more time a family spends together, the better the prospects for sharing quality experiences. For example:

Eat as a family. Parents and their children should enjoy fellowship around the table as much as possible. How sad it is when different members of the family eat independently at different times of the day, but how precious when they gather to share meals together. It strengthens the family bond. Children who grow up with a strong sense of family fellowship, especially at mealtimes, are more likely to retain that discipline of closeness with each other and their parents throughout their lives.

Worship as a family. At a critical juncture in Israel's history, as his ministry was drawing to a close, Joshua reaffirmed a great spiritual principle of family togetherness: "As for me and my household, we will serve the Lord" (Josh. 24:15). When a pastor takes the opportunity of family worship to affirm the family's loyalty to God's calling, like Joshua did, that family learns the value of keeping their lamps of faith trimmed and burning. In such situations, family worship binds the parents and children together in a covenant of faithfulness to God. In addition, family worship provides an opportunity to share personal experiences of faith; anecdotes about faith from relatives, friends, and brethren; and stories of faith written in Scripture, thus witnessing just as Joel declared, "Tell your children about it, let your children tell their children, and their children another generation" (Joel 1:3, NKJV).

Worshipping together is a blessing for any family. It provides an opportunity to share trials and victories, joys and struggles. Often family worship in a pastor's home gives the children the opportunity to learn firsthand the joys and struggles of pastoral ministry. Thus family worship is more than just a part of family life—it is at the very core of what it means to be a family, it bonds them all in spirit. A Christian home must be centered upon Christ, and as such it is filled with opportunities to worship Him. When that happens, the entire family will realize that no matter what else they do or do not do, the most important aspect that marks them as a family is that they are a worshipping family, submitting themselves to the lordship of Christ.

Organize family nights. Designate one night each week as family night. This is a special time for the entire family to spend time together in wholesome and fun activities. These may include: singing songs together, playing a table game, sharing humorous experiences from the week, making plans to volunteer together in the community, sharing a review of an interesting book or article read during the week, sharing what they enjoyed most in church last Sabbath, or writing a letter of congratulations, sympathy, encouragement, or prayer to a church member, thus strengthening the bonds between the pastoral family and the congregation. The main objective is that the night should take place regularly, be interesting, and involve the whole family.

After the activities on family night, all could go out to eat or have dinner at home. Going out to eat together as a family need not be restricted to family nights alone. It is good for the entire family to go out to eat whenever possible and as they can afford it. This should be planned with enough time ahead so the anticipation of it fills the children with joy even days before it happens. It refreshes their spirit as they look forward to the delightful event not far off. It is a real help in solidifying family life and creating memories they will one day narrate to their own children.

Additionally, for spouses who have their own parents living at a reasonable distance, make it a point to visit and/or call them regularly, and have the children partake in the experience. You may even plan to visit them on one of the family nights and let the fun take place there, or invite them over. In the case of a grandparent who is a widow or widower, it is especially important to draw them close. They were there for you once, and now you can be there for them. The wonderful anecdotes of elderly folks are a treasure. The children will learn of their heritage and gain a greater sense of belonging.

Go to church as a family. Cultivate the habit of going to church as a family and sitting together. It gives the congregation an example of a family united in worship. "The greatest evidence of the power of Christianity that can be presented to the world is a well-ordered, well-disciplined family. This will recommend the truth as nothing else can, for it is a living witness of its practical power upon the heart."[6]

Vacation as a family. Plan to have an annual family vacation, and if possible let it be to a different place, involving varied activities, each year. Start planning for it well ahead of time. Involve the entire family in the planning, even the youngest children, so they all have a sense of ownership in the travel and fun activities. The best memories I have from my childhood are the trips we took each year as a family, with varied fun every time.

The vacation does not have to be an elaborate one—just what would imprint fond memories that will remain for a long time. Less expensive, but just as fun-filled, would be to go camping, visit museums, tour historical sites, go to interesting towns, etc. You may even want to visit colleges and drive through the campus, thus planting the seed of higher education in the children. Whatever it is, escape from the routine and enjoy the vacation togetherness!

RELATE WELL TO YOUR SPOUSE

The most important person in your life, and the most supportive member in your congregation, is your spouse. Lean on your spouse, for you can count on her or him. Relate to your spouse and treat her or him with all the love and respect she or he deserves. More than anyone else, your spouse needs your support and encouragement. Here are some steps that I have found practical and successful in my marriage:

1. Pray for and with your spouse. The powerful scriptural description "bone of my bones and flesh of my flesh" (Gen. 2:23) is indeed a divine call to practice the oneness which is central in the relationship of husband and wife. The one singular and important activity that you as a spouse can engage in to make this relationship effective and sustaining is to join with your spouse daily and as often as possible in prayer. The couple who prays together finds that spiritual bond where both discover in each other what one needs and how that need can be fulfilled, and more importantly how they can complete together the ministry entrusted to them.

If you want to pray significantly for your spouse, stay in tune with her or his needs. A person who wants to support his or her spouse effectively through prayer must make time to know and understand her or him. That means you have to be in constant and meaningful communication. You need to know what is going on in her or his life, what she or he is doing and planning, what she or he thinks and feels, and what her or his needs are. Where there is a constant effort to understand your spouse, and where there is a genuine effort on your part to pray for and with your spouse, there will blossom a meaningful married life.

2. Publicly recognize your spouse's ministry. Often pastors believe that to praise one's spouse publicly reveals a self-indulging favoritism and sense of entitlement that should be limited, if not avoided. But actually, that is not so. A public affirmation of one's spouse should be seen as an acknowledgment of God's great gift to the pastoral team ministry, and as a recognition of the many sacrifices made every day for the pastor's ministry and the spiritual welfare of the congregation. Even if the spouse's greatest ministry may be in the home and not in the church, it is reason enough for public praise (Prov. 31:28).

3. Next to God, give your spouse first place. After your relationship with God, your spouse is your highest priority. When you do not put your spouse in first place in your life, in essence you are disdaining her or him, and it will not go unnoticed. She will feel overlooked and unimportant. It does not matter how you justify it; nothing is more important than your spouse. Would you ever think of starving your spouse of the food needed for sustenance? No! But you could be starving your spouse in other ways by denying emotional nurture. Pastors who neglect their wife can ever be qualified or empowered or fully fit to take care of God's people.

4. Privately show appreciation. Take advantage of moments to praise your spouse. Tell your spouse your appreciation. Nothing will encourage her or him more than for you to recognize her or his sacrifices, love, and devotion to the family. Affirm your spouse for who she or he is. Appreciating your spouse in season and out of season, with reason and even without reason, is one of the best energizing tonics you can give your marriage. However, be sincere and honest when showing appreciation. Flattery will not work. Also, appreciation must not fall victim to monotony. Vary your ways of showing it. Surprise your spouse with your methods: leave a note on the dresser, call just to say hello, send a bouquet of flowers whether or not it is a special occasion, and more so when it is. To let your spouse know every now and then how much she or he means to you and how thankful you are for being involved in your ministry, your family responsibility, and your personal growth is to arrive at the blessed summit of team ministry. Get there, be there, and enjoy it.

5. Ever train yourself to affirm your spouse. Solomon referred to the one he loved as "my beloved" forty times in the Song of Solomon.

> That choice phrase is packed with affirmation. It's a romantic expression, a call to rich friendship. Each time Solomon said, "My beloved," his words clothed her with dignity and value. What woman wouldn't flourish under such a constant stream of loving affirmation? It's important to remember that you are not doing these things to get something in return. Perhaps she will reciprocate in your language back to you, but that's not your goal.[7]

In the biblical language of "bone of bones, flesh of flesh," let that endearing term "my beloved" be reserved as the cement of love that keeps two lives together permanently, inseparably, to the glory of the Creator and the service of the Redeemer.

6. Surprise your spouse. You do not have to wait until a birthday or an anniversary to surprise your spouse. Flowers on a special occasion are nice, but I have found the ones my wife enjoys the most are those I send when she is least expecting them. Know what your spouse's favorite things are and surprise her or him with such a gift—anything she or he likes. You can even surprise your spouse by doing something wished for but unexpected. You do not need to spend a lot of money. It is fun to plan surprises! What is important is the element of a loving surprise and the joy of delivering the important message that you care.

BE BALANCED

Between day and night, work and rest, priorities of today and planning for tomorrow, evangelism and pastoral nurture, the demands of the body and the growth of the spirit, the wheel of balance must move on, neither tilting nor failing. A balanced life is essential to professional competence and fulfillment.[8]

However, one fact shared by most pastoral spouses is the daily struggle they face to balance family life and church life. "Balance is hard to find and more easily lost," says one pastoral spouse. "My husband and I have come a long way in our twenty-plus years of ministry. Over the years our lives and ministry have changed dramatically. With each change, there has been a need to re-achieve balance." Balance is an important issue in any pastoral family. "Achieving and maintaining balance in the parsonage is not a one-time event but a constant pursuit." Here are guidelines to help you keep your balance in the ministry:

Establish values. "While most ministry couples will acknowledge, at least cognitively, that family comes first, how do they maintain this priority when the demands of ministry have their lives speeding out of control?" It is good to decide early in ministry that when it comes to a "nose-to-nose choice between ministry and family," you would choose family. When your children are sick, you should stay home. You should communicate to church leaders or conference leaders that you cannot stay away from home for extended periods. More will be gained than lost in such decisions.

Explain to your congregations this issue of priority. Not only will they honor your decision, but they will follow your example of prioritizing family in their lives as well. The value we place on a balanced ministry that takes into account the needs of the family and the concerns of the church has far-reaching consequences.

Accept the realities of ministry life. Ministry is not a nine-to-five job. "Proper perspective in ministry is crucial. Having a heart for ministry is the key to perspective; understand that you are in the people business, and people take time and energy. It's more than a job; it's a passion for people." It is a calling to enable the weak, strengthen the tired, heal the hurting, and guide back home the lost. And ministry also, by its very nature, comes with a certain imbalance. There are no fixed hours and no fixed routines. We are on call almost every day; even planned days off are subject to change.

Another significant reality facing pastoral spouses is one of economics. Not all of them are able to work outside of the home, supplementing the family income. In such cases family finances can be tight, and it may not be easy to make ends. Being a one-income family means you would not have the lifestyle of your two-income peers. A new car or dream vacation may well be out of the question. But you have chosen ministry, and that is the value that should define your outlook. "Values determine priorities. Priorities keep you focused and balanced."

Be faithful to your calling. Ministry is a calling unlike all others. So the pastoral couple must resist the temptation of comparing their calling with anyone else's. When we make such comparisons, we always come up short. Ministry's demands may vary from person to person. Some pastoral spouses feel a calling to be a supportive role at home, caring for the children. Others feel impressed to support the pastor ministry in other ways. "Part of keeping your balance is being faithful to where God has placed you and being obedient to the things He has given you to do."[9]

Avoid extremes. We have already noted that the husband-wife ministry team does not have the option of neglecting the family in the name of serving the Lord. God does not expect that. To Him, serving and saving every individual in the pastor's family is as important as serving the larger family of faith and worship. God, in calling people to the ministry, does not expect the pastor to neglect one family for the other. The key is balance.

CONCLUSION

As we come to the end of this chapter, words such as "priority," "boundaries," "commitment," "togetherness," "protection," "involvement," "encouragement," and "balance" emerge to summarize the necessity of maintaining a strong pastoral marriage and family. Let God work in you and through you as you commit to making and keeping your family as a living witness to draw others into the family of God. To His glory and honor, your family can be a fountain of love, understanding, strength, and service.

Marriage is gospel ministry.[10] Home is that ministry's first arena. To succeed in both marriage and ministry, the marital union must be our first priority. Marriage is honorable (Heb. 13:4), and the solid foundation of ministry: "For if someone does not know how to manage his own household, how will he care for God's church?" (1 Tim. 3:5, ESV).

Keep in mind that your marriage is a living example of Christ's love for the church, both within your home and outside of it. As others observe how you treat your wife, the love of the Lord should be evident. It gives the Lord the opportunity to draw others to Himself as they observe your behavior.[11]

Hence your marriage is a powerful evangelistic tool because God uses it as a witness of His power to bring two different lives together to become one, creating harmony and peace. "Your marriage is another vehicle that God wants to use to draw others to Himself."[12]

As pastoral families, we walk along a path from which the end cannot be discerned. But we are never without hope of the amazing joy the destination will bring.

This life, therefore, is not godliness but the process of becoming godly, not health but getting well, not being but becoming, not rest but exercise. We are not now what we shall be, but we are on the way. The process is not yet finished, but it is actively going on. This is not the goal but it is the right road. At present, everything does not gleam and sparkle, but everything is being cleansed.[13]

We are all on the wonderful adventure and journey of life, and God is steadily transforming us into His image.

QUESTIONS FOR REFLECTION OR DISCUSSION

1. How do you demonstrate that family is your first ministry? Give some practical examples.
2. How do you spend quantity and quality time with your family during the week?
3. How do you place boundaries in your marriage and family?
4. Why are a balanced life and togetherness very important for the pastoral family?
5. How do you define a healthy ministry life?

ENDNOTES

[1] Ellen G. White, *The Adventist Home* (Nashville, TN: Southern Publishing, 1952), 102.

[2] White, *Reflecting Christ* (Washington, DC: Review and Herald, 1985), 167.

[3] White, *Counsels to Parents, Teachers, and Students* (Mountain View, CA: Pacific Press, 1913), 131.

[4] White, *The Adventist Home*, 102.

[5] *"Quality time" vs. "Quantity time" in Parenting*, www.focusonthefamily.com.

[6] White, *Testimonies for the Church* (Mountain View, CA: Pacific Press, 1948), 4:304.

[7] Dennis Rainey, "30 Ways to Love Your Wife," http://www.familylife.com/articles/topics/marriage/staying-married/romance-and-sex/30-ways-to-love-your-wife.

[8] This section includes information from pastoral wife Gail Johnsen; we incorporate her ideas with ours and with Ellen White. See Gail Johnsen, "Balancing Act in the Parsonage," *Enrichment Journal*, 2001, http://enrichmentjournal.ag.org/200102/108_balancing_act.cfm, accessed March 1, 2017. Used by permission.

[9] *Ibid.*

[10] This paragraph is adapted from "Husbands, Love Your Wives More Than Seminary," https://www.crosswalk.com/family/marriage/divorce-and-remarriage/husbands-love-your-wives-more-than-seminary.html, which is quoted in Wright, "The Ministry of Marriage: For the Pastor," accessed March 2, 2016.

[11] *Ibid.*

[12] *Ibid.*

[13] Luther Seminary, http://www.luthersem.edu/healthy_leaders/, accessed January 15, 2016.

— CHAPTER 8 —

PASTORAL CHILDREN: CHALLENGES AND BLESSINGS

"Your positive impact on the generations to come will be directly related to the ministry you have in that little place called home."—Jim George

God chose us to be parents. Parenting is not an easy task, nor is it always rewarding. It ever remains a challenge and blessing! While the parent-child relationship could be hard on us, it can be harder on our children. Many pastors' kids ("PKs") grow up with a deep resentment toward their parents, church members, the church organization, and sometimes even God Himself due to all the expectations placed upon them. I know this because Raquel and I raised two children of our own.

As a pastoral family, it is important to be aware of our own expectations of our children and the expectations of people in the church. Yet, not all children are the same, even within the same family. It takes time to really get to know them—their personalities, gifts, desires, joys, hopes, dreams, and uniqueness. For this reason, it is important to be aware of how our children think, who their friends are, how they relate to them and other acquaintances, how they process issues and choices, what makes them happy or disappointed, how they express their emotions, and how to build their self-worth.

Some kids are easy to relate to, and some are difficult. We try not to compare our children to each other or to other children; instead, we look at each one uniquely. With a loving spirit, understanding heart, and coherent action, we anticipate seeing successful results in their lives.

In our mission to educate and prepare our children for heaven, we must never give up hope. Look for the positives. Trust that the Lord has plans for them. Love them, spend time with them, listen to them, laugh and cry with them, believe in them, pray for and with them. Parenting is a joy and a challenge, though often a struggle. Raquel and I do not allow negative people or even ministry itself to rob us of our calling and mission: being parents under God's guidance.

> The work of parents underlies every other. Society is composed of families, and is what the heads of families make it. Out of the heart are "the issues of life" (Proverbs 4:23); and the heart of the community, of the church, and of the nation is the household. The well-being of society, the success of the church, the prosperity of the nation, depend upon home influences.[1]

LAY THE FOUNDATION

As Christian parents, it is our goal to see our children grow spiritually and develop a strong relationship with God. When the spiritual foundation is well established in their lives, we can rest assured that we are fulfilling our mission as parents. As a pastor, it breaks my heart when I see PKs leaving the faith. Being a pastor and having children, I have learned along the way how important it is to lay a strong foundation for our children when they are young. How can such a foundation be laid? Five significant steps may be noted: let children see in us the value of home life, prioritize family worship, emphasize on the importance of Christian education, make a commitment to shared values, and affirm children at all times and circumstances.

VALUE HOME LIFE

Pastors preach and listen. Yet although they spend a lot of time listening to the concerns of others, they often do not listen often or well enough at home. A bitter feeling often arises among children that "I am not important to my dad." Or, "These people dominate so much of my mom's time that she has no time for us." The resentment is often directed at the church, not at the parent. Resentment grows in PKs because there is no distinction between church and family, between priorities of "our time" with the parent, and the "church's time" with the pastor. Often—almost invariably—family time is stolen by the needs of the congregation, and the family is expected to deal with it.

One of the most effective ways to rectify that error and encourage PKs to appreciate ministry is for the pastor to adjust his or her calendar, apportioning time in such a way that the pastoral family and the church each gets due attention and time. It involves both embracing the children at home and reaching the lost in the community, worshipping with the family and preaching in the pulpit. In no way should the family feel ignored, neglected, or unmanaged. Love must begin at home before it can spread to the community of faith. Under no circumstances should ministry to the church come in the way of that "first love" of a pastor toward the spouse and children. A family who prays together stays together, and is an immovable strength in keeping PKs within the ambit of the church.

What does all this mean? To begin with, give due priority to family. During a family activity, turn off your phone or set it to vibrate mode, just like you do when you are about to preach or attend a meeting. If it rings just prior to the activity and you answer, make an appointment if your presence is sought, or say that you will return the call later that day or the next. The caller does not need to know why you cannot attend to them immediately. This gesture lets your family know they are appreciated and important to you.

In case of emergencies, family time may or may not need to be rescheduled. For example, there are emergencies that affect other persons but are not necessarily emergencies for you or your family. Assess the situation, discuss it with your family, and determine together whether or not you should continue with your plans to enjoy a special activity together, or postpone family time for a later date.

One of the ways we can help our family bond more firmly is to declare school holidays as family holidays. Non-pastoral families usually have many opportunities to be together at Sabbath services and other church events. The pastor's family does not always share this same privilege. So school holidays are an occasion to make up for these losses. This is a very important kind of expression of parental love and support much appreciated by our children.

PRIORITIZE FAMILY WORSHIP

Perhaps the family that finds it the hardest to have a regular family worship time is the pastor's family. Their schedule is often interrupted and many different activities separate them. Yet, when we set apart worship time at home, we are designating a special, specific time for the family. Thus we recognize that God is the center of the family. This is what family worship is all about—an affirmation of God's presence in the home. Christ is the divine head of our family, and when we as a family set aside a time to worship together, we acknowledge that God is our priority. All should be present, including the pastor, to meet with their heavenly Father, study His Word, place before Him their praises and petitions, and thank Him for His many blessings. The family altar is the one sure and enduring place to acknowledge God's leadership and seek His guidance: "God is our refuge and strength, an ever-present help in trouble. Therefore we will not fear" (Ps. 46:1, 2).

Children who learn to worship God in their early years learn to love and worship Him in later years too. The growing years of childhood are a great opportunity to establish the family in the faith and lead young people to personal convictions and decisions about what they believe and how they live. Our children and youth need a strong faith foundation and clear convictions to stand up against peer pressure, not indulge in wrongful activities, and resist the allure of misleading philosophies. They must understand their faith and know what they believe and why. They should learn to pray and intercede for others such as church leaders, pastors, evangelists, missionaries, those who are sick and carry heavy burdens, unsaved loved ones, neighbors, and fellow believers in need. Children who learn to pray openly at home will have no problem praying publicly as they grow. Only then Christian homes will nurture and develop young men and women who meet "the greatest want of the world," "the want of men [and women]— men who will not be bought or sold, who in their inmost souls are true and honest, men who do not fear to call sin by its right name, men whose conscience is as true to duty as the needle to the pole, men who will stand for the right though the heavens fall."[2]

VALUE CHRISTIAN EDUCATION

Raquel and I conscientiously made the decision to send our children only to Seventh-day Adventist schools because we understand the value and benefits of Christian education in our own lives. And today we are reaping the benefits of this important decision. We are profoundly grateful that we sent our children to schools where Christian values and attitudes were taught and emphasized. Our children grew up in a positive atmosphere where the visible effects of violence and immorality had not invaded the campus, and where moral values were held dear and spiritual ideals were promoted both inside and outside the classroom.

Christian education provides our children with a safe environment to grow: morally, spiritually, mentally, socially, and physically. In Adventist schools, our children spend a major portion of the school day under the influence of one or more Christian teachers. In the classroom, the teacher opens the grand vista of truth about God and the way He relates to human beings, all from the authoritative Word of God. The Christian teacher invites the students to experience an open, unashamed love of and service to Jesus Christ. Christian education offers a wholistic education that includes not only the "three Rs" of education (reading, writing and arithmetic), but also the higher reach of knowing God and His relationship with us. James Burn, author of *The New 3Rs in Education*, identified three different Rs important in education: respect, responsibility, and relationships. The benefits of such a comprehensive education offered in Adventist schools are far-reaching and long-term—another reason we sent our children to a Christian school. "The education that does not furnish knowledge as enduring as eternity is of no purpose. Unless you keep heaven and the future, immortal life before you, your attainments are of no permanent value."[3]

The Christian worldview foundational to Adventist education ensures that our children build their belief system, ethical structure, moral and spiritual commitments, and social responsibility on a rock of faith that stands firm, not on the sinking sands of relativism. We are ever thankful for Adventist education and its commitment to a philosophy of "harmonious development of the physical, the mental, and the spiritual powers," which "prepares the student for the joy of service in this world and for the higher joy of wider service in the world to come."[4]

Nurturing children with biblical truth is an excellent way to equip them for adulthood. Christian values taught in the Christian home and reinforced in the Christian school enable children to deal with a troubled world without succumbing to its problems—a good reason to send our children to an Adventist school.

When seeking the best for your children, obeying biblical guidelines is essential. Scriptural admonitions concerning the rearing of children in the Christian faith, found in such passages as Deuteronomy 6:5–7 and 2 Corinthians 6:14, can only be truly adhered to if children are taught in a Christian environment. Public schools cannot prepare a child for a fruitful, Christ-honoring life. In the Christian classroom, your child learns the biblical truth that is necessary for living a balanced Christian life.

Christian education may be costly, demanding a financial sacrifice and involving a geographical inconvenience, but the joy received from watching children grow academically, spiritually, physically, emotionally, and socially makes all the effort, time, and money worth spending.

COMMIT TO SHARED VALUES

God created humans as beings with values. Every sphere of human life involves values: spiritual, mental, physical, ethical, relational, intellectual, aesthetic, social, psychological, environmental, etc. Those of us who have heeded the call and accepted the value system of the Seventh-day Adventist Church find our values rooted in the Word of God and the saving power of Jesus. The third angel's message concludes with a value-oriented description of us as the last-day church: "Here are those who keep the commandments of God and the faith of Jesus" (Rev. 14:12, NKJV).

As parents and pastors, we have a primary obligation to instill in our children the central core of Christian values and bring them up in the knowledge of God and His expectations as outlined in Scripture so their values and lifestyle may be congruent with what God expects. "Start children off on the way they should go, and even when they are old they will not turn from it" (Prov. 22:6). Long before Solomon, as the community of Israel marched toward the promised land, Moses gave this timeless instruction:

> Hear, O Israel: The Lord our God, the Lord is one. Love the Lord your God with all your heart and with all your soul and with all your strength. These commandments that I give you today are to be on your hearts. Impress them on your children. Talk about them when you sit at home and when you walk along the road, when you lie down and when you get up. Tie them as symbols on your hands and bind them on your foreheads. Write them on the doorframes of your houses and on your gates (Deut. 6:4–9).

Emphasized here and in other scriptural passages is that teaching spiritual values to our children is non-negotiable. It implies that we understand what the term *spiritual value* means and then make it the core essential of our commitment in parenting. What does this involve?

First, teach spiritual values to children and help them develop a personal relationship with God. My children grew up with the knowledge that God is everywhere, but they also learned that He longs to live in their hearts. As parents, we need to help children feel connected to God. Talk with your children about God on a regular basis. Pray with them regularly and spontaneously. Teach your children that "prayer is the opening of the heart to God as to a friend,"[5] and they may approach God boldly and "with confidence" (Heb. 4:16). Help your children learn that Jesus is their friend, and He cares for them at all times.

Second, bring God into conversations with your children. Discuss the concepts of forgiveness, trust, patience, and faith. Every incident around the home—such as a glass dropping and breaking, a cut on the knee, not wanting to take a bath, not wanting to do homework, a quarrel with a neighbor's child, a poor grade in class—is an opportunity to bring God into the conversation. Let children learn that God is there to inspire, help fulfill life's responsibilities, show the high road of love and forgiveness, help them study well, and help them lead an exemplary Christian life. Let children know and experience that with God all things are possible, and without Him life has no meaning.

Third, and most important, set an example. Let children see how you use patience, faith, and trust in your life. Share with them the reality of your relationship with God. Pray with and for your children. Let them see you turn to God in times of stress, fear, indecision, and sadness. Let them experience with you your life of gratitude and dependence on God. Let them identify with you that God, who is your friend, is their friend as well. Hand in hand, heart to heart, mind to mind, lead your children to love God, obey Him, and want to be a part of His family.

AFFIRM CHILDREN AT ALL TIMES

Affirmation does not come easily. Affirmation consists of more than just words. As parents, our words and attitudes of affirmation have the power to build our children up and bring them into the fullness of life God has planned for them. In a world filled with stress, pressures, and fears, children need support and encouragement from parents—and they need to know how to affirm themselves.

I am not the "affirming parent" that I want to be—and that is partially why I am including here a few suggestions to help each one of us improve our relationships with family members, especially our children.

Praise children when praise is due. The question is not whether we should praise children, but how. Research has shown that praise is a high motivator to inspire children to work hard, learn better, explore further, and have a healthy outlook on their skills and abilities.[6] In addition, sincere praise that conveys realistic expectations can promote a child's self-motivation.[7] Just pause at an unexpected moment and say to your children, "Hey, I just want you to know I'm proud of you, and here are some reasons why!" Or tell them something like, "Great job!" Or encourage them with words such as, "Keep up the good work!" You will see instant rewards, whether it is a smile of satisfaction or a greater commitment to better performance next time around. Appreciation brings out the best in children, and even more so when parents move away from harsh criticism to encouragement of the positive.

We as pastors and parents must affirm our children as often as we can—not to boost their egos, but to show our confidence in them that they will choose what is right and appropriate, relate to others with love and kindness, resist the temptation to be self-centered and proud, be self-motivated to climb every mountain, and overcome every temptation.

Write notes. Write out the good qualities and successes you see unfolding in your children's lives. Even better—mail such notes to them. My wife always sends e-mails, notes, or cards to our children and other family members. She has a special ability to write notes of encouragement, affirmation, and motivation. Through such notes, you can express your unconditional love to your children for who they are, validate their wonderful gifts, and affirm their self-worth. Also reaffirm how great God's love is for them and how precious they are before God's eyes. Your children may not express their enthusiasm about your notes, or even acknowledge getting them, but be assured that your notes will affect their lives and always be remembered.

Understand their emotions. Children experience feelings of shame when they suffer social rejection; are unable to learn at the rate or level others expect; are defeated in competitions; are bullied, insulted, or taunted; or seek acceptance and approval from admired adults but are, instead, subjected to criticism or derogatory remarks. It has been said that everyone has a sign on their forehead that reads, "Make me feel important." This advice to employers reminds them that if they treat their employees with respect, the employees, in turn, will perform better. This saying holds true for all, including our children. There is something powerful about having "the way you feel" validated by someone in authority—even if circumstances do not change.

Let us always remember to value our children. We may not be able to give them their way, but we can let them know we understand how they feel. Such emotional understanding will help you know what your children need or want, as well as what they dislike. Being aware of their emotions helps you talk about their feelings more clearly, helps them avoid or resolve conflicts better, and helps you build better relationships with them.

Reward your children. Such a reward can be for no reason other than the fact that you are proud of their good efforts in some area. Rewards are healthy for kids because they learn that privileges and extra incentives must be earned. According to Virginia Shiller, a psychologist and author of the book *Rewards for Kids,* rewards can help parents teach their children new habits. Rewards let them know that you, as a parent, highly value and esteem them. Treat them like you would treat someone very important in your world, praising and/or rewarding their effort, persistence, and accomplishment.

Express affection. Studies have shown that higher self-esteem, better parent-child communication, and fewer psychological and behavioral problems in interpersonal relationships are linked to warmth and affection between parent and child.[8] As a parent, the affection I feel for my children is limitless. I want them to grow up knowing they are deeply loved. Each moment brings a new chance to say, "I love you"—not just with words, but also with actions.

Many parents today do not know how to express love and affection toward their own children. Some people grew up in a family environment lacking affection, and may not realize that life can be happier and more pleasant if only affection is felt and expressed.

> Parents should keep the atmosphere of the home pure and fragrant with kind words, with tender sympathy and love; but at the same time they are to be firm and unyielding in principle. If you are firm with your children, they may think that you do not love them. This you may expect, but never manifest harshness. Justice and mercy must clasp hands; there must be no wavering or impulsive movements.[9]

Teach self-discipline. One of the primary tasks of early childhood is to develop self-discipline. Parents often find themselves correcting their children for interrupting, being wild, not following instructions, or not controlling their hands or mouths. Such tasks require self-discipline and self-control. Young children are impulsive by nature. Some children have biological and other factors that increase impulsiveness. Part of the solution for impulse control is to teach them self-discipline. A child armed with self-discipline and self-control has a tremendous asset for addressing life's challenges, and resolving many relational and personal problems.

While parents have a right to expect their children to obey their instructions, they must remember that it is their responsibility to make the children understand the reasons behind restrictions, expectations, and standards. Any parental restriction or expectation carrying the weight of arbitrary function or authority does not foster in children a loving understanding of parental authority. If a parental goal is to teach children the values of self-discipline, must not the methods of such teaching be rooted in love and reason? Children who grow up in legalistic environments in which the parents simply bark out harsh orders seem to obey only as long as parents are watching. When parents turn their back, these children often choose to act in rebellious ways.

Point out the positive. Helping children develop a positive self-concept may be one of the most difficult tasks of parenting or teaching. I have discovered that I was quick to point out the wrong things my children are doing, even though I correct them in a loving way. Unfortunately, I was not quite as quick to notice when they were playing quietly, working hard, or getting along with one another—which are acts and behavior that deserve notice and appreciation. We need to train ourselves to be aware of our children's good choices, and encourage them verbally with words that reinforce positive behavior.

Positive parenting demands bringing out the best in children by listening and understanding, praising and encouraging their efforts, noticing and rewarding good behavior, and doing things together that you both enjoy.

THE PK ADVANTAGES

While growing up as a PK has many challenges for the pastoral couple and the children, it has many advantages as well. It is to these advantages that the family should turn in their training and upbringing of children. Dwelling on the negatives and the problems of being a pastor does not help. Give better reasons for your family standards. Help them focus on the positive. Let them see the many advantages pastors' children have. Some of those advantages are the wealth of spiritual exposure, increased opportunities to grow, special recognition, and, above all, a spiritual heritage that is theirs to possess.

SPIRITUAL EXPOSURE

Being a PK provides the opportunity to see the miracle of growth in God's work and be an active witness and participant in its joys. When our children frequently participate in our ministry, they see faith at work in the lives of others. When God moves in our lives and in the life of the congregation, our children experience firsthand how the Holy Spirit works in ministry and evangelism. A firsthand experience to such workings of the Spirit leaves a lasting mark on our children and creates opportunities for their spiritual growth and nurture. Nothing has been more gratifying in my ministry than seeing the Holy Spirit working not only over the congregation but also over my children.

There are times when we as pastors see our children seated in the front row drawing doodles during our sermons, and we may think they are not absorbing anything from what we preach, but we may be surprised to find how much they learn. Pew sitting for hours has its own rewards. Many PKs have a better knowledge of the Bible and doctrine than other children. In addition, theology taught through hymns and choruses will stick with them even as they reach adulthood and serve as a source of inspiration, comfort, and gratitude.

Sometimes family time can blend with ministry to the benefit of both. Children growing up in a pastor's home are privileged to have firsthand knowledge and experience of the struggles and victories, the hopes and joys, and the private and public roles of ministry that mark the lives of pastors. They are challenged by their parent's commitment to ministry, and encouraged to rely on God's guidance just as their parent shows how helpless he or she is without the strength that comes from above. Blessed is the pastor's home where the parents leave an example of spiritual strength and total reliance upon God both in their ministry and family life.

INCREASED OPPORTUNITIES

Being a PK brings opportunities that other children do not. While there may be some elements of the PK life that pastoral children complain about, often times those are the same elements that they appreciate as adults. But if such PKs participate in church life and their family's ministry, they will find themselves with increased opportunities to discover their giftedness in areas of music, hospitality, verbal communication skills, and leadership abilities. Some of today's well-known Christian music artists were raised in ministers' homes.

There are other advantages to being a pastor's child as well: special scholarship provided by the church, participating in pastoral retreats and special events, the opportunity to develop leadership and administrative abilities, and the advantage of growing in personal dignity and social skills.[10]

SPECIAL RECOGNITION

During their childhood and as they grow into their preteen years, PKs are objects of affection and endearment to church members. The local congregation and community tend to shower them with special recognition as part of the pastoral family. PKs enjoy knowing that most members know them by their first names. They, for the most part, enjoy standing by their parents and greeting church members, and playing the part of small-time celebrities. At times members give them special privileges and sometimes gifts. Many PKs also feel blessed to have a local support network in the congregation: church members watch out for them, help them, protect them, and take care of them. PKs often acknowledge the spiritual and social support they receive from church members, and express their gratitude for the special blessings they receive from God as a result of church members' prayers on their behalf.

A SPIRITUAL HERITAGE

Growing up as children of a pastoral family, PKs inherit a rich spiritual heritage. The value of their character formation, the love of their exemplary parents, and the sense that their family enjoys a special blessing as part of obedience to the call to ministry give them a special opportunity in life. Most of them agree that in their home life, their parents taught them about the Bible, guided them in the Christian life, and were examples of how to live by faith.[11]

Yes, pastors' children can be distinctive and make a difference as they grow in the grace and knowledge of the Lord Jesus Christ. We need to seek God's guidance to raise our sons and daughters as arrows from the quiver who pierce the darkness and turn many to righteousness. Let us not leave them behind by neglecting them or failing to set an example of love and care.

QUESTIONS FOR REFLECTION OR DISCUSSION

1. Why do some children like to be PKs and others do not?
2. What are the blessings and disadvantages PKs have?
3. Why is a Christian education so important?
4. Why are expressions of affection so significant to children?
5. How can parents reward the positive behavior of their children?

ENDNOTES

[1] Ellen G. White, *The Ministry of Healing* (Mountain View, CA: Pacific Press, 1942), 349.

[2] White, *Education* (Mountain View, CA: Pacific Press, 1952), 57.

[3] White, *Fundamentals of Christian Education* (Nashville, TN: Southern Publishing, 1923), 191.

[4] White, *Education*, 13.

[5] White, *Steps to Christ* (Mountain View, CA: Pacific Press, 1948), 97.

[6] Mojdeh Bayat, "Clarifying Issues Regarding the Use of Praise With Young Children," *Topics in Early Childhood Special Education* (2011): volume 31, issue 2, 121–128.

[7] J. Henderlong and M. Lepper, "The Effects of Praise on Children's Intrinsic Motivation: A Review and Synthesis," *Psychological Bulletin* 128 (2002): 774–795.

[8] Martha J. Cox, "Parent-Child Relationships," in *Well-Being: Positive Development Across the Life Course*, ed. Marc H. Bornstein et al. (Hillsdale, NJ: Lawrence Erlbaum).

[9] White, *Adventist Home* (Nashville, TN: Southern Publishing, 1952), 434.

[10] Molly K. Rankin, "Shepherdess: Pastors' Kids Are Different," *Ministry*, December 1981.

[11] Bill Carmichael, "Preachers' Kids: Their Unique Challenges and Battles," *Enrichment Journal*. We have adapted and included several ideas from this throughout this chapter.

CHAPTER 9

THE UNHAPPY SIDE OF MINISTRY

"The past cannot be changed. The future is yet in your power."
—Unknown

We have all heard stories of pastor's children walking away from the faith. I am not a pastor's kid (PK), but my wife and our children are. My father was a literature evangelist, so I was not in the church's spotlight as my children have been. There are obvious pros and cons of growing up in a pastoral home. There is no doubt that PKs face unique challenges.

Working with pastoral families around the world, I have the opportunity to observe how many of them interact with their children. Our children are our greatest joy and, at times, our greatest frustration and heartache. Let's be honest: there is no such thing as the perfect family, the perfect parent, or the perfect child, including the ones in ministry. So let us consider some potential problems or challenges that contribute to the sad and painful reality of why some PKs go off the path their parents, well-wishers, and, above all, God desires for them.

MINISTRY BEFORE FAMILY?

Some pastors forget, ignore, or minimize the biblical warning: "If anyone does not know how to manage his own family, how can he take care of God's church?" (1 Tim. 3:5). Meetings every night, phone calls during suppertime, long hours planning sermons, and serving in ministry duties outside of the home may create resentment for spouses. However, for children this could be devastating. They see their parent constantly prioritizing ministry over spending quality time with them. But they do not have the emotional maturity to separate their parent's behavior from the beauty of our Savior. Hence, they may become resentful of the church, and everything in ministry that is dear to their parent, all because they feel overlooked, neglected, and taken for granted.

So let us discuss some problems we may have allowed to surface and solutions to save our children from blaming God and ultimately turning away from Him.

Be present being away. If you have to be away, it may be beneficial to let your family members accompany you and share your ministry opportunities. Your children need to believe that you would rather spend time with them than with the people of the church. Children will harbor negative views toward ministry if you put the needs of everyone else ahead of your family's needs. "Great good done for others cannot cancel the debt that [the minister] owes to God to care for his own children."[1]

A pastor in the church must first be a pastor in the home. This requires more than a subjective sense of calling. A pastor is not perfect, but the one who aspires to be a pastor must consistently demonstrate a general godliness in the home in addition to other areas of life.

God, as the model in ministry, is accessible to His children. Of course, His omnipresence ensures a level of accessibility we are unable to achieve. Even so, we can learn greatly from our heavenly Father's desire to communicate with His children. A parent cannot reflect God well when distracted on the Internet, checking emails, taking calls, watching television, reading books, or preparing a sermon. If we are to be godly parents who manage our homes well, then we must learn to turn off cell phones and laptops and be at home mentally when we are home physically. As the saying goes, "Wherever you are, be all there." To our family, our interactions with them are far more important than our sermons on Sabbath morning.

Unrealistic expectations. Pastors can place excessive expectations on their kids because the church wrongly puts these expectations on the pastor's family. One pastor's kid said, "It was very stressful being a PK because everyone judges you differently, like you're supposed to be perfect. And then if you did mess up, it was a bad reflection on Dad. We were told that by my parents often."

Such expectations are not limited to behavior, but also include the child's participation in church functions. The pressure on kids to help their parent look good in front of their congregation can be overwhelming on them.

Yes, church members may have expectations about how they think preacher's kids should be. But as a lifelong pastor I am convinced that, for my children, the most important issue should be the expectations we, as parents, have for them. What do we feel it means to live out our faith within the family? This matters far more than what the deacons or elders or members think. If our children are confident of our love and know our good expectations, then teaching them to live within our boundaries will help them develop an appropriate attitude toward life in the pastor's home. Any Christian home should be built upon the principles set forth in God's Word. If you are struggling with expectations as a pastoral family, maybe it is time to give your home a reality check and see if some expectations need to be adjusted to God's Word.

Hypocrisy. Children grow bitter when watching a parent live an insincere lifestyle. Nothing is more harmful to our children than to live in a home where we say one thing in the pulpit and act another way at home. Parents leading double lives is one of the most damaging things our children face. Ministers often feel pressured to lead perfect lives. We all know it is not possible, but many are still tempted to play this role. In an environment like that, children assume that the faith we proclaim is just an act, and eventually walk away from us, our home, and the gospel we preach because they have not seen the real gospel. They may say, "He treated my mother awfully. He ruled the house with an iron fist, never with grace. I knew most of the stories in the Bible, but I never learned from observation how to apply them to my life."

Ellen G. White gives this precious counsel: "God designs that in his home life the teacher of the Bible shall be an exemplification of the truths that he teaches. What a man is, has greater influence than what he says. Piety in the daily life will give power to the public testimony. Patience, consistency, and love will make an impression on hearts that sermons fail to reach."[2]

As a pastor, if you have failed in this test of consistency, your family, more than anyone else, needs to hear you confess your shortcomings. This is problematic for a pastor's family.

Integrity always matters, but if a Christian leader wears two faces—one in public, one at home—the gospel is dishonored and pople are eventually disappointed. Then do not be surprised if somewhere down the line they walk away from the gospel, disillusioned, and you are left to face the decisive question, "Where is the flock that was given thee, thy beautiful flock?" (Jer. 13:20, KJV).

But do not fear. Take heart. God knows we are a needy people, and the people we minister to need to know it too. It is out of our needs that we see God work. When we show we too are in need of God's help, mercy, and grace, the people who follow our ministry will see the reality of God working in us. And most importantly, our children need to see God working in us as well.

A parent, not just a pastor. You are called to be a pastor, but PKs want not just a pastor, but a parent—someone who loves them and their family, plays with them, protects them, makes them laugh, hugs them, pays attention to what they say and what they need, take an interest in their schoolwork and friends, and teaches them practical life lessons. They want committed love and warmth. They want a parent who is not a workaholic, one who is involved in their lives, in their ups and downs. They want a full-time parent— not necessarily 24/7 presence, but a life of total commitment to the work of being a parent.

It is inappropriate to ask your congregation to love, sacrifice, and exercise passionate gospel living while you neglect your own family. Your children will have no place for your pastoring if they miss out on your parenting.

Some children sadly conclude, "I am not a rebellious, spiteful PK because I am not really a PK. I am just a guy whose parent happens to be a pastor." Sure, having a pastor-parent is different, but I think one of the biggest reasons PKs get so rebellious is that they don't really have a parent—they have a live-in, full-time pastor who treats the kids more like members of the congregation.

Because such a backlash from our children can be real, it is necessary for you to clearly understand the great responsibility you have in your home— your spouse and children. Our homes must not be exchanged for our pulpits. In our pastoral lives, we need to keep in mind that sermons are an effective way to communicate biblical truth to our congregation, but to our family it takes much more: a sermon in flesh and blood, born and pursued in love, a permanent feature within the walls of our homes and the hearts of our family. So being with and for the family, and not just delivering powerful sermons from the pulpit, will help build a stronger and more enduring relationship with them. With such a home PKs cannot wander away.[3]

Guard your conversation. Pastor, protect your children from unnecessary information. This is true not only when children are young but especially later in their teen years. Do not discuss in the presence of children anything negative—any bitter experience you may have had with a church member, church leader or the conference; or anything you consider to be bad examples or injustice. Do not share discussions of discipline you may have had in the church. Guard your speech and the information you share so that children grow in a positive atmosphere of gratitude and thankfulness. Exposing your children to experiences of injustice or negatively within the church or from church leaders may cause them to become bitter against God or the family of God.

Pastors have to deal with all sorts of problems within their congregation. An effective, growing church is more like a spiritual hospital. People's lives are messed up in sin. Ugly things happen. Sin in one form or another and issues such as divorce, addiction, depression, and bitterness—all cross our path. If ministers bring this "dirty laundry" home and discuss it in front of their children, they do them a great disservice. It is important that our children do not pick up our grievance or frustration. They should not be given either the burden or the right to hear about other people's problems and sins. Believe me, they will see plenty of problems without us calling attention to them.

Sometimes others may be upset with you as a pastor. All pastors know that many of the things said against them are only partially true, if not totally false. These are issues you need to handle by yourself or with the counsel and help of your spouse. Be careful that your children do not become part of the disagreement and take up your defense. When your children do that, it can affect their lives not only mentally and emotionally but can even be a catalyst to eventually deny their faith. God will give us His grace to deal with those who come against us. Leave the kids out of it.

Abandonment. Abandonment of children does not happen only when one of the parents physically moves out and ceases to have contact with their children. PKs can feel abandoned when our ministry and lives are too busy with other things or are out of sync with theirs. Saying, "You matter to me more than everything else in the world," and then letting everything else eat up all of our time, tells our children that our words are hollow and meaningless. Being there means we are not only physically there, but our focus, affection, and interest are there too. We must be real enough to occasionally kick up our heels and have a good time with our children.

Authoritarianism. Authoritarianism in the church is one of the most serious problems it confronts. The issue is also present in some pastoral homes—another reason why some PKs abandon their faith.

Authoritarian pastors who think of God in terms of legalistic obedience and see Him as vengeful and arbitrary. Such pastors do not take time to know and relate personally to the God of the Bible. The Word of God speaks of God as One who is love (1 John 4:16), full of grace and mercy (Eph. 2:4, 5), our help and sustainer (Ps. 54:4), gracious and righteous (Ps. 116:5), the strength of our hearts (Ps. 73:26), our burden bearer (Ps. 68:19, 20), our eternal forgiver (Mic. 7:18, 19), and One who will remember our sins no more (Heb. 8:12). Pastors who speak and preach about such a God of mercy and tenderness can in no way be authoritarian and legalistic. Their parishes as well as their home will taste the goodness of the Lord every day and live within the understanding and forgiving nature of God.

An authoritarian church tends to control almost every aspect of the church member's life. It wields the law as a weapon of terror and instrument of judgment. Such a church tends to intrude into every aspect of believers' lives: what they believe, how their homes should be structured, and how they should conduct their social and economic lives. Members are told what they should do with their money and how they are to eat and dress. They are told whom to vote for, what to read, what to watch on TV, and what kind of music to listen to. I am not against biblical instruction on such details of life, but I am not comfortable with being intrusive and authoritative in the lives of my members, telling them what they should do or not do, rather than focusing on my own relationship with God, who is able to transform and save.

Religion rooted in authoritarianism leads people to keep and value irrelevant traditions, formalism, and legalism. It should come as no surprise that this kind of religion damages people emotionally, psychologically, and spiritually. Many people who live this kind of religious experience or practice are frustrated with their spiritual lives and may leave the church, never wanting to return again. They are content to be free from a church that is legalistic and authoritarian, and whose expectations are not rooted in the Bible but upon traditions and the desire to wield power and authority, far from the biblical mandate of grace, mercy, and tenderness.

Authoritarianism also tends to show up in family structure and government. Here too, it happens when the parent—in patriarchal ideology, always the father—wields absolute control over his spouse and children. Thoughts, actions, decisions, and the desire of other family members are all subject to his will. Future plans; activities; clothing worn; and even, to some extent, the food eaten are governed by the father's decision, spiritual authoritarianism, legalistic radicalism, and perfectionist expectations—according to the father's definition of perfection, his tyrannical will.

In my own life, I grew up and was trained under the influence of this kind of unbalanced religion. I attended a very controlling and strict elementary school, academy, and college. As I entered the ministry and began pastoring churches, I promoted and practiced authoritarianism in many ways in my church and home. How could I do anything else? It was all that I knew. It was all that was ever modeled to me.

When you have no knowledge about what is right or what it means to be a real Christian, all imbalanced things in religion make sense. Only when you are truly converted can you look back and say, "Wow! I was on the wrong track all that time—believing and practicing things not in tune with the gospel." But once I realized how wrong I was in my authoritarian life and ministry, and turned my way around, how sweet and liberating life and ministry turned out to be for me and my family.

DANGERS LURKING IN THE HOME

It is said—perhaps whimsically—that there is a great likelihood that the child of a teacher will become a dropout, the child of a police officer will become a delinquent, and the child of a pastor will become an atheist. But is that really true? For a possible answer, consider the dangers lurking in pastoral homes.

The prodigal in our homes. We all know of numerous teachers with kids who excel academically. Most police officers have law-abiding children. And most pastors have children who are engaged in following Christ. The problem lies in expectations, and the expectations for pastoral families are usually high. As pastors, we sometimes fall into the trap of expecting that our child will become the next Billy Graham or Mother Teresa. But when a prodigal emerges in the parsonage, many pastors are overwhelmed and even somewhat embarrassed. They fear that the prodigal's presence will be perceived as a poor reflection of the pastoral family's performance. Parishioners, too, can become perplexed and judgmental.

Certainly, Scripture cautions pastors of this danger lurking within their homes. The apostle counsels that a pastor "must manage his own family well and see that his children obey him, and he must do so in a manner worthy of full respect. (If anyone does not know how to manage his own family, how can he take care of God's church?)" (1 Tim. 3:4, 5).

Paul's words are not an expression of a management philosophy, but simple, inspired commonsense advice pertaining to the relationship of a pastor's management of the home and leadership of the church. A pastor who does not keep the house in order, ill-treats his or her spouse, and lets their children wander into the wilderness of indiscipline and a lifestyle that is opposite of the Christian norm can hardly be expected to care for the spiritual nurture and growth of a church with members experiencing different problems and needs.

Thus the home becomes a critical base for measuring a pastor's management responsibility. A child can be obedient and treat his parents with respect, while his heart is not at peace with God and his life far away from Him. An authentic spiritual relationship with God is not something we can create or control in our children. It is for them to discover on their own and grow in grace and the knowledge of the saving power of God. And this is the way God has ordained how a Christian home ought to be.

Struggling with faith. The journey toward authentic faith is a lonely one, and this is particularly so in the pastor's home. Compared with other children in the church, it may take pastors' kids longer to surrender their hearts to Christ and be harder for them to walk in His way. Children growing up in a pastor's home may find it difficult to separate the cultural Christ from the crucified Christ. The cultural Christ governs Bible study and prayers only as a routine, not as a way to walk closer to God; faith is something to possess but not a life aglow to share with others; and what one believes is a statement of doctrine, not the transforming power of life and practice.

The crucified Christ, on the other hand, demands of every member of the pastor's family, including children, to give up self decidedly, radically, and totally, and obey the commands of Jesus by having a faith worth dying for. The call of the crucified Christ demands that He take priority over family culture and personal preoccupations. To follow the crucified Christ and become fully committed to the ministry of the church becomes even more difficult as children enter into the perilous stage of adolescence with its natural urge to challenge authority and question the priority of the Spirit. Sometimes a prodigal detour, although disconcerting for pastoral parents, is the path certain children need in order to make their faith real. Prodigality may come as an easy sidetrack to pastor's children, but a home founded on the principles of enduring love, law, and grace, rooted and established on the crucified Savior, provides a safe haven for the growth and nurture of a pastoral home.

Having said that, is there still something we, as pastors, can do to ensure that our children remain within the safety of God's embrace? From our own experience—the ups and downs, my wife and my struggles and victories as lifelong partners in ministry—I can share a few thoughts that helped us groom our children in the Lord's way: (1) Under the grace and power of God, we try to live a life in alignment with what we believe and preach. Contradiction between faith and practice on the part of either parent is a sure way of confusing growing children about how they should walk. (2) We pray for them and pray with them. When they see the importance of prayer in their parents' lives, and the home life, they too will experience the power of the bended knee. (3) We have family worship regularly. That is the first altar children should experience—the altar where self-sacrifice is taught, God's Word is read, and the great scriptural lessons of God's love and grace, sin and the power of the gospel, promises for the present and hope for the future, and other great truths are studied together as a family. (4) We try to be an example in word and deed, in the home and public, in preaching the Word and practicing love, in looking forward to heaven as God's promise, and in making the home here a heaven on earth. With these done, embrace your children constantly in God's grace and love, and God will bless them as you fulfill your parental responsibility.

TIME FOR REFLECTION AND ACTION

Pastors' children are not destined to become prodigals, but the number who leave their faith is growing at an alarming rate. Are pastors sacrificing the best of their life and ministry for the salvation of others while neglecting the salvation of their own children? Pastors should aspire to be the shepherds of all the flock entrusted to them, both within the confines of their homes and within the enlarged tents of their church families. The home should be a model of a loving, grace-filled, healthy center of Christian nurture and growth, even as the pastor builds and serves the larger community of faith. Neither service—of the home or of the church—can be at the expense of the other. Ministry in the truest sense embraces both, for the Lord who created the Christian home is also the one who founded the church. Within that perspective, pastors must live out certain inescapable responsibilities.

Face reality. Just because we love God does not guarantee that our kids will also. Encourage your children to genuinely explore what they believe in and why, without any pressure. What our children believe and how they choose to live their life in conformity with their faith must come as a result of personal exploration and choice, not of parental or societal pressure.

Even given that freedom and the best of parenting children may, for a time, walk away from the faith they were raised in. But what happens next may be the determining factor in whether those children eventually return.[4] Every home must face the possibility of a prodigal child, and every home must also have the certainty of a waiting parent with an embrace of love. After all, Jesus compares the Father's love for us with a father who runs with joy to meet the prodigal son who "was dead and is alive again; he was lost and is found" (Luke 15:24). Every pastoral parent must face the reality of death and resurrection within the precincts of his home. Our love and acceptance of our kids is never more important than when they rebel against us. It is then that they will truly see the God who searches after and even dies for them. And it is then that we need to model the God who forgives and pursues us for the sake of our children.

Pray for them. Pastors spend a lot of time praying for their flock, but their own family needs to be at the top of the prayer list. Solicit the prayers of a few trusted friends to join you in bringing your children's spiritual needs to the foot of the cross. Prayer allows us to look past our child's behavior and see the person who God is in the process of developing. White says, "God will hear you pray. He will love to answer your prayers. But He despises your prayers while you neglect your duty to your children and then pray Him to do the work for them."[5]

Do not feel guilty. As parents, remember even if you do everything right in terms of Christian parenting, your children can still make bad decisions and choose to go astray. Try to discern the kind of fall your prodigal's behavior denotes. Often the prodigal has not violated some biblical principle, but has given way to a personal preference or conviction that may be contrary to your expectation. In any case, true "love is patient, . . . is kind. . . . It always protects, always trusts, always hopes, always perseveres" (1 Cor. 13:4–7). If you exercise that kind of love, you need not feel guilty, but rather exercise hope and patience that the child who wandered away is only a prayer away from home.

Understand spiritual warfare. The enemy knows that one of the best ways to sidetrack pastors is to attack their children. The enemy can use well-intentioned church people to drive them deeper into a prodigal lifestyle. Our role is to protect our children from the enemy. God's promise is sure and certain:

> The race is not to the swift, nor the battle to the strong. The weakest saint, as well as the strongest, may wear the crown of immortal glory. All may win who, through the power of divine grace, bring their lives into conformity to the will of Christ. . . . In view of the issue at stake, nothing is small that will help or hinder. Every act casts its weight into the scale that determines life's victory or defeat. And the reward given to those who win will be in proportion to the energy and earnestness with which they have striven.[6]

Examine your family practices. Sometimes we make prodigals out of those who are not really prodigal at all. Sometimes children engage in prodigal-type activity simply to get our attention. It could be that the compliant child may actually be farther from God than the prodigal. Behaviors rarely happen in isolation. Think about how each member of the family affects the other. Maybe we as parents are somehow contributing to our child's rebellion and their stepping out of the church. An apology from you may be the catalyst to soften that child's heart. Also, the problem may not necessarily be spiritually rooted, but may be a reflection of some emotional struggle, such as a social crisis or depression.

Such times in the life of your children demand a closer relationship to show that you care deeply for them, and that you are ever there to share their emotional strains. This may be the time when you need to say no to that extra committee meeting or Bible study or evangelistic campaign so you can spend some extra time with your child, perhaps go on a trip that you promised your son or daughter in an effort to reconnect. In certain cases, it may be necessary to ask your conference to let you have a home-based sabbatical to address issues with your family. It is during moments like these that God's promise is so reassuring: "Cast all your anxiety on him because he cares for you" (1 Pet. 5:7).

When you notice that your children are in need of emotional sustenance and spiritual vigor, perhaps that's the time for deep self-reflection as a family. With the help of your spouse or a trusted family member, you may want to ask yourself: What practices and/or beliefs would your children inherit from you? Do such practices and beliefs reflect God's ideal for a pastoral family? How does your life as a pastoral couple consistently reflect the Christian ideals you expect to see in your children as they grow into mature adults? Where else could you be more intentional about passing faith on?

Share your experience. Think of your own spiritual journey and you will no doubt recall that you spent many months, if not years, processing what it meant to be a committed follower of Christ. How much time did you spend in the pig pen before you came to your senses? Sharing your story in age-appropriate ways with your children could demonstrate how one repents and turns to God.

Guard your marriage. Having a prodigal can put enormous stress on a marriage and drive a wedge between husband and wife. Issues surrounding a prodigal can occupy all of your talk time. But your prodigal child needs your marriage to be healthy. This may be the best time to intensify the investment you make in your marriage, so that you and your spouse can build a joyful family that provides a safe haven to young people who face their own challenges to their faith life.

Get help. Sometimes a family needs an outside perspective to get the warmth back in a relationship that has grown a bit cold. Do not be afraid or embarrassed to find a professional counselor who can help. Even pastors can lose their objectivity. A good friend can also help you see clearly, while a counselor can help you understand the deeper issues at hand. Another person can help your children in a more appropriate and effective way. God is always using other faithful Christians to bless members of His spiritual family in a very special way. So work hard to restore a warm relationship between you and your child of any age. That special relationship is a significant force in your child's faith development, and it is never too late to attain it.

Believe they will return. We need to exercise those three greatest virtues of faith, hope, and love as they relate to our prodigals. Keep the faith, never lose hope, and love them deeply. Our kids need us to be a personification of God's grace, mercy, and unconditional love. Whether you have a young prodigal or an adult prodigal, maybe you need to go to them, open your hearts, ask for forgiveness where needed, and provide love, assurance, and acceptance so that the son or daughter who has wandered away may return home and feel embraced by the faith of their parents. Maybe some of these children are hurt, bitter, angry, or disillusioned. Perhaps they need to hear from you how much they are loved in spite of all the mistakes you made while serving in ministry.

If you are still raising little PKs, ask the Holy Spirit to show you where your children are adversely affected by your actions. Humbly ask for their forgiveness—even if they are in preschool. Then bring up a generation of PKs who see their parents in need of a Redeemer and trust in the grace of God more than they fear the accusations of a congregation.

Nothing breaks the heart of a pastor and spouse more than one of their children walking away from the faith. There are many pastors today with broken hearts. Those of us who have not had this bitter experience may not understand how painful it can be. Whether we understand the full gravity of that pain or not, the true nature of pastoral ministry demands that we extend the warmth of our fellowship and the assurance of our prayers to those families who continue to suffer the agony of living with the knowledge that their children, their own flesh and blood, their object of love and concern, have become aliens to the house of faith.

Pray for such struggling parents. Pray for those prodigal children that they might see the heavenly Father waiting for their return.

> Through the goodness and mercy of Christ the sinner is to be restored to the divine favor. God in Christ is daily beseeching men to be reconciled to God. With outstretched arms He is ready to receive and welcome not only the sinner but the prodigal. His dying love, manifested on Calvary, is the sinner's assurance of acceptance, peace, and love.[7]

Finally, for parents of prodigals, recognize that religion and love are not the same thing. A lot of parents personalize their child's rejection of religion as a rejection of them as parents. That is easy to do because religion means so much to such devout parents. They want their children to have the benefits of the same life of faith they enjoyed. They want to see their children in heaven. Such desire is laudable, but parents must not confuse religious conformity as a condition for extending parental love; likewise, lack of religious conformity on the part of the children must not be taken to mean a lack of love for parents. A Christian home should always be a place of unconditional love—love that loves the unlovable, love that ever forgives, love that ever waits with that accepting embrace God extends to the prodigals.

LOCAL CHURCH LEADERS AND PKS

I hereby make a heartfelt call to all local church leaders: elders, deacons, deaconesses, and department directors. Be aware of the spiritual needs of all the children attending the church. They are loved by God, and you have the opportunity to be patient and love, counsel, and guide them. In particular, help by keeping an eye on the pastor's children on Sabbaths while the pastor is busy conducting service, and their other parent may be a little overwhelmed by an equally busy schedule on this day. Too many pastors' children are casualties in the spiritual warfare. After seeing the inner workings of the church, many do not want anything to do with the Lord or His people. As a teenager, I almost walked away from my faith because, instead of being loved by my fellow Christians who were adults, I witnessed hypocrisy and injustice in my church.

Those children running around among us are precious to God. One day they will no longer be six and four years old; they will be twenty-six and twenty-four. In the meantime, they are watching and listening to you. And through their observation, they are deciding if the gospel is real. Jesus said, "By this everyone [including these children] will know that you are my disciples, if you love one another" (John 13:35). What will they say about your church when they are adults? What should you, as a church leader, do to help such children walk with Christ?

Care for the pastor's children. Saturday is a busy day for the pastoral family, unlike that of any other person's workday. While the pastor is ministering, the spouse is parenting alone. The pastor's children are often the first ones to arrive at the church and the last ones to leave. Church leaders can minister to the pastor's family by giving their children love, talking with them, and fellowshipping with them. PKs are a blessing. If you are blessed to have a pastor with children, love your pastor by loving the children. It might mean being patient with them, being supportive of them, or just remaining silent—praying for them to your heavenly Father.

Share your concerns with the pastor. As a shepherd of my family, I wanted to know when my children acted up. I appreciated any report I received from an adult who cared for me and my family, and knew that children will be children, prone to make mistakes. They did not look at my children as PKs, only as kids.

Honor them. As children grow older they need to see that their pastoral family is respected. The pastor's children will soon figure out that their family does not drive the newest car or take the nicest vacation, but if others express respect in words and actions for the pastor, the children's respect for their parents will increase. Those who show respect to a pastor and pastor's children can make a substantial difference in the life of the PKs.

Avoid the spirit of criticism. Every group of people will have problems. Issues will need to be sorted out. But know that young people are watching how adults handle problems. As a teenager, I was keenly aware of conflicts and hypocrisy in my church. Make sure you keep any negative comments among just the adults. Take any issues privately to the leadership. Do not make sniping comments to young people or within earshot of them.

Support the pastor's family. Children need their father. But many pastors will be tempted to neglect their own families to meet the unending needs of the church. Condemning the pastor will not solve the problem. But as a local church leader, you can encourage your pastors to care for their families. Are they taking their days off? Are their vacations uninterrupted? And never demand that they minister to your crisis at the expense of their own family.

Growing up as a pastor's child is not easy. It is full of unique challenges and struggles, which the kids did not choose. With so many children leaving the church as they grow older, it is so important that all church leaders take time to befriend the PKs and intentionally minister to them.

CONCLUSION

Your family is a flock within a flock. Your first calling is to manage your own home and, along with your spouse, care for the souls given to you. Congregations come and go, but our families will remain. Take the same care of your children as you do for your larger flock. Parents are often the instruments by which a child is brought to the saving faith of Christ. Listen to your children. Take time for them. And when you see your time being dominated inordinately by outside concerns, speak to your elders and cut back. We cannot save our children, but we can certainly reduce the number of outside influences that may affect their view of the church.

Above all, pray for your children. But more than this, show them you also are a sinner in need of grace, imperfect, looking to Christ as the Author and Finisher of your own faith.

QUESTIONS FOR REFLECTION OR DISCUSSION

1. What could you say to help a pastor who has a prodigal child?
2. In your opinion, why are PKs leaving the church?
3. What are the real and unreal expectations the church members have of PKs?
4. How can the local church leaders help the children of the church love God?
5. Why is it important that children not hear adults criticize and gossip?

ENDNOTES

[1] Ellen G. White, *Gospel Workers* (Washington, DC: Review and Herald, 1915), 204.

[2] *Ibid.*

[3] Barnabas Piper (blog, Twitter), Nashville, TN.

[4] Vern L. Bengtson with Norella M. Putney and Susan Harris, *Families and Faith: How Religion Is Passed Down Across Generations* (New York: Oxford University Press, 2013), 189.

[5] White, *Manuscript Releases*, Volume 9 (1990), No. 758, 323.

[6] White, *The Acts of the Apostles* (Mountain View, CA: Pacific Press, 1911), 313, 314.

[7] White, *Selected Messages* (Washington, DC: Review and Herald, 1958, 1980), 1:178, 179.

CHAPTER 10

SEASONS IN PASTORAL MINISTRY

*"Be aware of what season you are in and give yourself
the grace to be there."—Kristen Dalton*

Every season in life has its challenges and opportunities, and each minister must reach out and grasp the possibilities and promises of each season. The call to ministry is a call to live and serve, study and preach, pray and worship, mourn with those who mourn, rejoice with those who rejoice, and be a faithful witness to the One who has called you to be the bearer of His Word. "Preach the word! Be ready in season and out of season. Convince, rebuke, exhort, with all longsuffering and teaching. . . . Be watchful in all things, endure afflictions, do the work of an evangelist, fulfill your ministry" (2 Tim. 4:2–5, NKJV).

The demands of such ministry expect the same faithfulness, sense of responsibility, and sense of fulfillment from all in varying seasons of life: from the single to the married, from the young to the retired. Regardless of the challenges of the station a minister should be able to reach out for the ultimate source of strength, saying, "I can do all things through Christ who strengthens me" (Phil. 4:13, NKJV), and then look forward to affirm, "I have fought the good fight, I have finished the race, I have kept the faith" (2 Tim. 4:7).

SINGLE IN MINISTRY

Being a pastor is not the most easy or popular vocation in life. And being an unmarried pastor is even more rare and challenging. Even the apostle Paul, who perhaps did most of his pastoral and missionary work as an unmarried man, encouraged the concept of a pastoral family when he wrote, "If anyone does not know how to manage his own family, how can he take care of God's church?" (1 Tim. 3:5). Preparation for ministry in Bible colleges and seminaries includes discussions and guidance as to how to choose a life partner who will be a strength to the pastor and involved fully in team ministry. Rarely are courses taught on how to function as an unmarried pastor. "Seminaries train pastors on how to navigate the challenges of ministry and family life, but they often leave out conversations on what to expect as a single pastor. The church can be an isolating place for single people."[1] In many places the church is not sensitive to the spiritual and emotional needs, and social requisites of single people in ministry. What's more, some denominations penalize single ministers by delaying their ordination because of their marital status.

Another challenging issue for single pastors is work-life balance. In ministry, that balance is often discussed within the context of marriage and family. Thus, single pastors may feel that work-life balance does not apply to them, but it does. They need to be aware of work-life balance in the way they approach of personal health issues and the challenges of ministry, fostering supportive platonic friendships, and building community relationships within the church. Work-life balance applies to everyone, but often this principle is applied to ministers with families rather than single pastors.[2] The corollary of such a situation is that more professional counseling and assistance is available to married pastors; significantly, none or very little assistance is focused on single pastors.

Moreover, single ministers face the issue of whether their singleness is permanent or transitory. Are you called and gifted by God to remain single for a lifetime? You should consider this prayerfully, and seek an honest and thoughtful answer.

CHALLENGES OF BEING SINGLE PASTORS

There are vital areas of ministry that present challenges to a single pastor. For example, counseling young people seeking to establish a Christian home of their own, couples in need of counseling for marital issues, or parents in need of parenting skills. A pastor who is a spouse and parent has experience that helps him relate to these advice seekers, but a pastor who is single does not. However, having said that, we do not take the extreme position that singleness disqualifies one from offer that type of relational and family advice. The Holy Spirit is the ultimate Equipper and Enabler of ministry; thus all things are possible—including ministry by single men to a congregation made up of both single and married folks—though the situation would be challenging.

Society often imposes additional challenges—false or imagined. For instance, a man who remains single beyond a certain age may be labeled with a stereotype questioning his sexuality. But per divine counsel, we are not to judge anyone, nor render false testimony by spreading rumors.

The God who calls one to ministry also gives the grace to live a life that brings glory to Him, whether single or married. Dealing with sexual desires is a matter of the heart, and God can empower a person to deal with such issues. After all, did He not order Jeremiah to remain single (Jer. 16:1, 2) even though celibacy was rare among both prophets and priests in the Hebrew community? Jeremiah chose to forego the joy of family life due to the urgency of God's task and the distress of the times. In the history of God's people, many single men have devoted their lives to ministry, honoring God with singleness of purpose in body and mind.

While marriage does not guarantee relational faithfulness in ministry, singleness does not mean a deficiency in character expected of those in ministry. How, then, shall we ensure that ministry under all seasons and conditions is to the glory of God and an exemplary shepherding of His flock? Perhaps the following will provide an answer: "Who has the heart? With whom are our thoughts? Of whom do we love to converse? Who has our warmest affections and our best energies? If we are Christ's, our thoughts are with Him, and our sweetest thoughts are of Him. All we have and are is consecrated to Him. We long to bear His image, breathe His spirit, do His will, and please Him in all things."[3]

SINGLENESS IN 1 CORINTHIANS 7

The apostle Paul does not address, neither in support of nor against, the issue of single men serving as pastors in 1 Corinthians 7. Yet Paul's counsel has been actively debated by the church and, consequently, the marital status of pastors has been widely misunderstood, and often the message's central issue is missed. But what is even more troubling is that while Paul does not address the issue of single men serving as pastors, many cite this message in support of or against it. While the apostle is not arguing as to whether it is right or wrong for single men to serve in ministry, he is giving wise counsel regarding how the marital state affects life and ministry experiences, especially in the context that "time is short," and "this world in its present form is passing away" (vv. 29, 31). What's more, the time in which Christians live calls upon them to "live in a right way in undivided devotion to the Lord" (v. 35). To better understand what Paul is saying regarding unmarried pastors, let us consider the context of the passage, starting with a biblical understanding of marriage.

In the Bible, being single is not the ideal. The Creation account clearly states, "It is not good for the man to be alone" (Gen. 2:18; cf. Matt. 19:4–6). Marriage is to be honored by all (Heb. 13:4). To teach against marriage is to fall into the trap of following "deceiving spirits and things taught by demons" (1 Tim. 4:1–3). Practically, however, for some people there are seasons and reasons that provide exceptions to the rule of marriage. Paul clearly explains this in 1 Corinthians 7, and his words are as true and timely as ever. Those called to remain single for a season or a lifetime in order to devote themselves unreservedly to the ministry of the one who has called them will find in His Word, as did Jeremiah, a reservoir of divine strength and stability to accomplish their mission without any distraction or deviation (Jer. 20:9). Their calling will be sure and certain, pure and chaste, undiluted with the cravings of the flesh but fully focused on advancing the interests of God's kingdom.

Such is Paul's counsel to those who choose to be single. However, Paul is realistic: he knows that some may not find it easy to remain sexually pure and spiritually holy in a state of singleness. In such cases, the apostle advises that "they should marry, for it is better to marry than to burn with passion" (1 Cor. 7:9). Later in the chapter (v. 26) Paul encouraged singleness because of the "present crisis," which may have meant the impending persecution at the hands of Nero and/or a deadly famine that had been prophesied (Acts 11:28), or, more importantly, imminent end-time events leading to the second coming of Jesus and the urgency to take the gospel to the ends of the world. Such context adds weight to the cause of being single and totally committed to the cause of the gospel. A person so committed can fully concentrate on the gospel mission without being diverted or burdened with the need to care for a spouse and children. However, Paul adds that ministers already married should not seek divorce, implying they should not abandon the responsibility of caring for a family, for to marry or remain in marriage is not a sin (1 Cor. 7:26–28).

It is important to remember that Paul is not elevating singleness to a status of preference, but providing grounds for singleness under some circumstances. In this way, if some are called to remain single and wish to serve in ministry, nothing should prevent them from doing so. There is nothing in being single *per se* that should prevent a person from being a minister. After all, pastors, in general, even if they are married, function independently for the most part. Ministerial functions such as home visitation, Bible study, counseling, hospital visitation, and baptismal study and preparation, are often performed by pastors individually and not joined by their spouses. Therefore, all should work in ministry based upon the sincerity and seriousness of their calling, not their marital status, in order to have access to the challenges and joys of ministry.

Having said that, we should also keep in mind the advantages that married pastors have. Congregations are made up of children, adolescents, youth, young adults, single men and women, married couples, families with young children or teenagers, middle-aged families with an empty nest, and senior citizens. Ministry to these groups may be better served by married pastors, and even more so by the team ministry of the pastor and his wife. Many member issues in the average church relate to marriage and parenting, and mentoring and counseling young people. Such issues are best dealt with by married leaders (1 Tim. 3:4, 5; Titus 1:6; 2:3–5) who also have experience raising and living with their own children.

ADVANTAGES OF SINGLENESS IN MINISTRY

In ministry, being single offers its own advantages to the unmarried pastor. Two such advantages may be noted: time and focus.[4]

Time. Ministry takes time—for study, sermon preparation, pastoral visits, home visitation, evangelism, and other essential pastoral responsibilities. Personally speaking, I often think of the amount of time I had at my disposal when I was single, and how speedily this time shrunk when I got married. When I was single, I found myself with plenty of time to invest in many essentials of ministry. Regarding sermon preparation, for example, I had lots of time for study, sermon construction, and revision. Even the day before the delivery of the sermon, I had time to go over the sermon again, make it a little better, search for a better illustration, refine the wording of an important passage, make the exposition a little more thorough. Being single I also found it possible to choose proper applications in the sermon to address those critical moments in the life of the congregation. Singleness also allowed time to build effective working relationships with elders, deacons, deaconesses, and heads of various departments within the church, such as Sabbath School, youth ministry, Pathfinders, and community services.

However, when I got married, I immediately found myself in a position where the resources of time and talent demanded a split attention between ministry and family. Family life is a holy calling: to nurture the marital relationship, care for one's life partner, and provide for the material needs and social aspirations of a growing family take time and demand resources. The time available for ministry is drastically reduced when one gets married. Our time and energy are finite, and when ministry and marriage need to be equally cared for, the task of equally meeting the challenges of both is not easy. Certainly, when I was single I slept more and studied better. Scheduling work activities was easier than after I got married. Plus, being single meant having fewer domestic expectations and duties.

Focus. In 1 Corinthians 7, Paul speaks extensively about Christian life as being in continual tension between living in this world and living in preparation for the world to come. Among the many areas of tension a Christian faces, the apostle focuses on married and unmarried persons and their relationship to Christian living and witness. For example, a single person does not have the responsibility of caring for a spouse and children. Paul argues that those who are not married can give undivided attention to the call of the gospel. Thus "he who is unmarried cares for the things of the Lord—how he may please the Lord" (v. 32, NKJV). The point to note is not that it is better to be single, but that the tensions of life are reduced for single persons, thus enabling them to be substantially more focused on ministry and church affairs. Yet nothing in life should distract the unconditional commitment the gospel commission demands of its ministers, whether single or married.

By saying all of this, we do not suggest that it is better to be single in ministry. Married pastors find their own strength and stability, can reach farther, and have better communication in ministry than single pastors. However, what we wish to emphasize here is that being single in ministry can be a calling with a particular blessing in that it offers more time and better focus.

MARRIAGE AND MINISTRY

While unmarried pastors have advantages in terms of time and ministerial focus, that does not mean a married person is necessarily less effective in pastoral ministry. In fact, one can argue that a married couple can have an effective team ministry like Aquila and Priscilla (Acts 18). The experience of being married helps the pastor and spouse to effectively minister in such areas as family and children's ministry and marital counseling. This can propel the couple's ministry, whereas a single pastor may not be readily competent in those areas.

Moreover, a married pastor has the opportunity to build and develop a home that in itself can be a powerful witness to Christian goodness and grace.

> As the minister and his wife faithfully do their duty in the home, restraining, correcting, advising, counseling, guiding, they are becoming better fitted to labor in the church, and are multiplying agencies for the accomplishment of God's work outside the home. The members of the family become members of the family above, and are a power for good, exerting a far-reaching influence.[5]

When I got married, I discover several additional advantages in my ministry. Of these I particularly cherish two important dimensions: maturity and spiritual growth, and emotional breadth and empathy.[6]

Maturity and spiritual growth. I begin with this advantage because it comes as the most pronounced in my preaching responsibility and the most effective in my relational ministry. Marriage demands that I walk toward spiritual maturity. As I walk this journey, I find many challenges to overcome and many relational hills to climb. Each day, I face moments of uncertainties and pangs of tension which, if met appropriately, can make me a person who receives due respect from my life partner. In turn we, as a couple, can be an example to our congregation of what Christian marriage and witness ought to be. A person will not last long in ministry or marriage without growing in the desire and ability to please his or her spouse (1 Cor. 7:33), and making every effort to minister together to the congregation. In that relational strength and united service of love lies not only marital maturity and spiritual growth but also the power of team ministry. The highs of marriage are greater than anything I experienced in my singleness. Yet I am regularly challenged and confronted with marriage's demand to die to self, live for your spouse, and as a team and pastoral family give ourselves unreservedly for the service of God, the strengthening of the church, and its pastoral agenda in the community.

When I was single, I was as free as a bird. I could get up when I wanted, eat what and when I chose, set my own agenda, go to sleep when I wanted, and choose to prepare my sermons as I pleased. But marriage's demands took over my self-imposed, self-serving schedule. It restructured and balanced my life and ministry as two became one. Marriage for me became a powerful biblical calling (Gen. 2:24). As a result, selfishness was replaced by selflessness because now my choices took into consideration the preferences of my wife. That awareness brought change, spiritual growth, maturity, and a host of other qualities that enhanced my ministry. Marriage taught me what years in the seminary could not. The better you are as a spouse, the better you are as a pastor, for pastoring at its core is serving. "The greatest among you will be your servant" (Matt. 23:11).

Emotional breadth and empathy. Pastoral ministry deals with many delicate issues in life—often related to marriage and parenting. While it is possible that single pastors can adequately apply God's Word to all of life, they may still struggle without the blessings that come from the marital union: the wisdom that comes from shared experience in prayer, Bible study, and team ministry; the relational experience of a two-in-one life and the certainty and empathy of a focused journey. The joys and sorrows of marriage give an emotional depth and breadth to the pastor and spouse in their ministry to the congregation. Marriage helps the pastor instinctively identify the problems couples in the congregation may face, and the pastor can minister to them based on personal experience. Singleness may have its own unique emotional pains, of which God can still use, but the married pastor has a broader and deeper emotional experience of humanity and its relational complexities.

I am happy to be married. And I am also aware that there are many single pastors who find joy in serving the church. Too often these debates regarding pastors and marriage force us to choose sides. But the Bible does not rate them; it honors both. We should do so as well. I would urge churches and search committees to evaluate candidates for pastoral ministry on their character, gifts, and maturity—not only on their marital status.

YOUNG PASTORS

Be it the words of wisdom spoken through Solomon, "Remember now your Creator in the days of your youth" (Eccl. 12:1, NKJV), or the words of inspiration expressed through Paul, "Let no one despise your youth, but be an example to the believers in word, in conduct, in love, in spirit, in faith, in purity" (1 Tim. 4:12, NKJV), God has a certain and definitive role for youth in His ministry on earth.

> Upon Christian youth depend in a great measure the preservation and perpetuity of the institutions which God has devised as a means by which to advance His work. Never was there a period when results so important depended upon a generation of men. Then how important that the young should be qualified for this great work, that God may use them as His instruments! Their Maker has claims upon them which are paramount to all others.[7]

The Adventist Church is ever blessed by an army of trained and sanctified youth who carry its evangelistic, pastoral, and missionary work throughout the world. It is amazing to see these valiant groups of young pastors working in ministry with great fervor and idealism. Many of them take up their initial appointments highly motivated and filled with enthusiasm, firmly believing they are going to make a difference, doing what others before them have not done. Youthful enthusiasm is exciting.

I look back to my own experience. How many mistakes I could have avoided in the early years of my ministry if pastoral support would have been available to me to fine-tune my motivation and orient me with the right instructions, training, and correction. What a Spirit-filled ministry young pastors can give to churches today if only they have mentors such as Timothy had in Paul: "Don't let anyone look down on you because you are young, but set an example for the believers in speech, in conduct, in love, in faith and in purity" (1 Tim. 4:12). Paul says that young pastors like Timothy should "flee from all this [evil], and pursue righteousness, godliness, faith, love, endurance and gentleness [and be ready at all times to] fight the good fight of the faith" (1 Tim. 6:11, 12). A life of such total commitment to the gospel calling matches the highest expectations a church could have of a pastor. Our life, not our sermon, needs to spell and proclaim what we say and believe. Paul is telling Timothy that pastoral leadership is a mirror that reflects God's character. God cares about "who" we are more than "what" we say we are!

The following are some suggestions on how young pastors can avoid the most common pitfalls in their youthful journey in pastoral ministry.[8]

Spiritual priority. Your spiritual health matters to your church. Your pursuit of Christ affects your people. You know this, of course, but do your daily life and schedule reflect it? As a pastor, your life-blood, power, and strength come from the time you spend with God. Trying to accomplish your ministry without doing this would be the biggest mistake in your life and ministry. It is comparable to sailing out into the ocean and never coming to shore to replenish your supplies. How can you help a soul adrift in the vast sea if you yourself run out of provisions? Likewise, you embark on a voyage by being a pastor. You must daily refuel by spending time with God in Bible study and prayer in order to renew your spirit, and have the strength, power, and wisdom to be a true and effective pastor. Spending time with God is crucial for your congregation, and it starts with you. So take time every day to invest in building your relationship with God. Only then can you effectively guide people to Him.

Learn from others. Coming out of college, young pastors often think they know everything. Some have a spirit of arrogance and self-confidence, and assume that those who lack formal religious education have nothing to teach them. This is a grave error. Do arrogant pastors know the Spirit of God? Does God need them to impact hearts, enlighten the minds with wisdom from above, and plant the seed of unconditional love in their souls? Of course not. The Holy Spirit is actively working with everyone and a wise pastor will listen to the holy lessons many humble souls can teach them. Having the attitude that a degree from a seminary renders them superior in knowledge to those placed under their care is dangerous.

Such pastors belong to a group the Bible terms "Laodiceans." "You say, 'I am rich; I have acquired wealth and do not need a thing.' But you do not realize that you are wretched, pitiful, poor, blind and naked" (Rev. 3:17). Learn to tread with humility and openness early in the ministry. Fellowship with your people knowing that, as far as God's love is concerned, they are on the same level as you. Learn how to communicate with each individual in sharing the Word of God. Understand their deepest feelings, minister to their needs, and reach out and bring them into the embrace of God's grace. But most importantly, learn how God has dealt with them before you came along, and be amazed. Listen to their wise counsel and learn.

Know your church. Strive to understand the spiritual and inner dynamics of your congregation. Listen to their stories. Trust the church leaders who have been there longer and know the church better than you. Retired pastors and seasoned elders have years of experiences having gone through things you could never imagine. They are a great source of wisdom. Therefore, be humble and seek to befriend them. They have already paid the price of wisdom with their many years of experience in the pastorate.

Your willingness to learn who your congregation is as a people will show them that you do care and will open them up to trusting your leadership. Refrain from rushing to fix what you perceive as a problem right away. Build rapport with them in the beginning, then they will trust your counsel on how to make corrections.

Beware. Stay alert regarding the traps that can destroy your ministry, especially the two big traps—love of money, and lust.

Be cautious in dealing with church finances, and as a rule do not handle financial issues independently. While you are to do everything possible to promote church finances and stewardship, you must not assume that it is your responsibility to take actions regarding spending money. Every church should have a set norm on budgeting and spending. Money is not evil. It is the love of money than can bring you down.

Lust can destroy your life and ministry. Watch yourself. Make sure you never put yourself in a position of moral compromise. I do not know anything that has destroyed more young ministers than moral lapse. Heed this counsel:

Let not Christ's ambassadors descend to trifling conversation, to familiarity with women, married or single. Let them keep their proper place with becoming dignity; yet at the same time they may be sociable, kind, and courteous to all. They must stand aloof from everything that savors of commonness and familiarity. This is forbidden ground, upon which it is unsafe to set the feet. Every word, every act, should tend to elevate, to refine, to ennoble.[9]

Preach with care. Paul's charge to young Timothy on the priority and substance of preaching is ever relevant to all pastors, particularly to young ones: "In the presence of God and of Christ Jesus, who will judge the living and the dead, and in view of his appearing and his kingdom, I give you this charge: Preach the word; be prepared in season and out of season; correct, rebuke and encourage—with great patience and careful instruction" (2 Tim. 4:1, 2). While the apostle's instructions are all we need, it is appropriate that young pastors take note of some dos and don'ts pertaining to preaching: (1) Preach the Word after thorough study and prayerful preparation. Homiletics teachers often say that one minute of preaching requires a minimum of one hour of preparation. (2) Make your sermons Christ-centered, and let each preaching occasion be a time when the congregation can meet the Savior afresh. (3) Be cautious when preaching on certain subjects in which you may not have the expertise, skill, and finesse; such subjects include marriage and sexuality, successfully raising children, and emotional health. It takes time, study, and experience for you to preach on such subjects. When such subjects need to be included in your preaching calendar, it may be well to invite a senior or retired pastor with experience in those areas. (4) Respect the sacredness of the pulpit. Do not spend pulpit time on irrelevant stories or jokes. (5) Never forget that the preaching hour is a time when the Holy Spirit mediates the mind of God through His Word so that God's people can have a wholistic experience in worship, prayer, study, and fellowship.

Be flexible. When we are young, we think we know it all. We are dogmatic and stubborn in our convictions. Many times we dismiss instructions from our parents until we stop listening to their counsel altogether. What do they know? Their ideas and views are so antiquated. But life soon takes over and teaches us a lesson or two, until one day when we need to make a difficult and important decision, and we reach out to mom and dad for advice. Hurray! Maturity has set in.

To all young people I give this advice: Not everything can be viewed through black and white lenses. Be open minded; listen to varying opinions. Learn from the hard lessons that others experienced and want to share with you, before you damage your reputation more than necessary. Why do I say this? Because I realize that the older I get, the less I know.

Therefore, young pastor, do not pretend to be a know-it-all. Do not be rude, censorious, critical, cruel, or insensitive in either word or deed. Instead, be flexible and understanding in your convictions when principles are not involved. Be loving and kind, willing to learn from those who sincerely care about your success. Their wisdom will crown you with many blessings.

Be zealous with knowledge. "Zeal without knowledge is not good; a person who moves too quickly may go the wrong way" (Prov. 19:2, NLT). Young pastors tend to show great passion and compelling vision in ministry. There's nothing wrong in having such enthusiasm, but one needs to exercise caution in how and on what this enthusiasm is expressed. Ministerial enthusiasm without an adequate knowledge base of ministry practices and without an appreciation for cultural differences may lead to misunderstandings in the congregation rather than unity and appreciation. This concern is particularly apt when we face the tendency to speak about some church traditions and cultural issues as biblical principles and scriptural commands. Search for understanding, because zeal without knowledge is not good.

This problem is more evident when speaking about issues regarding cultural dividers in multicultural congregations, and what procedures to follow in dealing with church practices and social activities where differences may exist. In such cases it is best for young pastors to not take an unyielding stand, but work together with the congregation and seek the strength and guidance of the Holy Spirit to preserve the unity of the church and fellowship of the congregation.

Aim to serve, not perform. It has been said that in any vocation—be it teaching, preaching, health sciences, social services, or politics—during the first half of our service we are driven to succeed, while in the second half we are driven to be significant by leaving a legacy. Young pastors are no exception. In their early years of ministry they tend to be more concerned with appearance and performance or the opinion of others than with the centrality of reaching the hearts of their listeners with the message God has for them. To focus on that message requires a high degree of commitment to their own spirituality and prayer-connectedness with God. It may take years to realize this accomplishment, but without that nearness to God, ministry cannot be complete. Hence the importance that ministry be focused on service, not performance. The pulpit is not a stage for theatrical performances, but a point from which radiates God's love and care. As Paul counsels Timothy, "Do your best to present yourself to God as one approved, a worker who does not need to be ashamed and who correctly handles the word of truth. Avoid godless chatter, because those who indulge in it will become more and more ungodly" (2 Tim. 2:15, 16).

Be prepared to meet all expectations. When they finish their academic training, pastors do not yet have all the competence they need to meet the expectations of their ministry. These will come unexpectedly, challenging their expertise and skill, and can be overwhelming. In their effort to resolve issues, they may get into embarrassing situations because of inexperience or ignorance, or both. Thus it is all the more necessary for young pastors to be in touch with three vital sources of strength that allow them to anticipate and prepare for challenging situations: (1) Continued study of what is expected in ministry beyond what you learned in the training program; such study resources can include drawing strength from a deep study of Scripture and other relevant literature, keeping in touch with experienced pastors, and knowing and relating with members of the congregation. (2) A strong, faith-oriented prayer life, pleading with God to give you the spirit of discernment and spiritual insight to find biblical foundations and answers to help you meet challenging expectations. (3) A strong reach-out experience so that you can build a wide circle of friends and colleagues with which to fellowship, receive counsel, and get help in overcoming difficult expectations.

Because you may feel challenged by unknown and higher expectations, "let no one despise your youth, but be an example to the believers in word, in conduct, in love, in spirit, in faith, in purity" (1 Tim. 4:12, NKJV).

Be prepared to face family stress. Family and related issues can be a major cause of ministerial and relational stress in your early years as a pastor. Finance and family budget are the most obvious stress points, wherein your spouse may have to seek work outside of the home to supplement the family income. Then, when a baby comes along, one or both spouses becomes less available to meet their daily ministerial duties. While most church members understand the responsibilities of parenting, some are unwilling to adjust their expectations for you and your spouse. Soon you will find yourself constantly choosing between the needs of your family and the people you are committed to serve. "The minister's duties lie around him, nigh and afar off; but his first duty is to his children. He should not become so engrossed with his outside duties as to neglect the instruction which his children need."[10]

Seek in ministry God's approval. The apostle Paul well defines whom we should please in our ministry—not humans but God. He says: "Am I now trying to win the approval of human beings, or of God? Or am I trying to please people? If I were still trying to please people, I would not be a servant of Christ" (Gal. 1:10). However, one common trap that young ministers fall into is the false notion that success in ministry lies in their ability to keep everyone happy—church members, local church leaders, conference administrators, and visiting leaders. The young pastor seeks to be recognized for his leadership in many areas of ministry—preaching, evangelism, church administration, church growth, stewardship, and so forth.

Additionally, young pastors also want to be perceived in a good light by their leaders, especially during their evaluation process for ordination. Hence there is pressure from all sides to please people. Trying to do all of that and gain the approval and goodwill of everyone is a hopeless task. When ministers seek to please everyone, their families are usually neglected. Spouses and children are expected to understand because, "after all, we're in this together." But there is no real togetherness when the minister places the demands of others before the needs of the pastor's own family.

In the early years of ministry, some pastors get discouraged when their dreams seem far from fulfillment. As a result, sadly, some of them leave the ministry. Such need not be the case. If young pastors take time to study, pray, and fellowship in accordance with biblical instructions, it will result in their close and abiding connection to the Lord. Then their experience will lead them to have a healthy and spiritual ministry where its center and focus is not self but others, not self-glory but God's glory, and where the blessed hope of the soon coming of our Lord will be the consuming focus of preaching, worship, prayer, and study.

SENIOR PASTORS

We are people of seasons, as it is declared in Ecclesiastes. There is a time for every season under heaven. It is not different in ministry. Each season of ministry has its responsibilities and opportunities, but in each God is ever faithful, and His work keeps marching forward.

Maybe you are in a place of ministry that is very fulfilling and fruitful, or maybe the ministry seems to be slowing or diminishing. You may be wondering what you are doing wrong and why things are not working as well as they used to. This is the perfect time to evaluate what is going on. You may be at a plateau or you may be losing ground, so you must stop long enough to ask God to enlighten you as to what is happening and what He wants you to do at this point. Perhaps you just need to adjust your ministry a bit. Otherwise, it may become stale. You always need to stay flexible as you lead since it is up to the Holy Spirit to direct your ministry.[11]

What if you are in the "autumn" time of your personal life and ministry? Your life routine is changing. Perhaps you do not like changes. You may now have an empty nest, or perhaps you are about to retire. You do not want to leave the busy summertime of life when you are very active and involved. Or maybe this makes you think, "Wow, now I have time to breathe again and take it easy." But maybe God wants you to reevaluate that as well. Maybe He wants you to say, "Wow, now I have more time to serve Him!"[12]

This is a perfect time to refocus on the most important things God wants you to participate in. After a growing season in the summertime and the fruits that often appear in the autumn of life and ministry, it is now the moment to revisit God's call to serve and the purpose of your ministry. Let Him speak to you on all levels of your walk and service as you advance through the changes of autumn.

If you are a senior pastor, navigating through this transition well is even more important. The strength of your church, but more importantly your family, cannot afford to be neglected during a season of pastoral growth or change.

Prayer is what sustains us in times of transition. Senior pastors have the responsibility to be an example of steadfast faith even in challenging times. While no pastor is perfect, the way they may act in a difficult season is indicative of both their faith and ability to lead. That is why turning to God is so important. When you lift up your burden to the Lord, knowing that He is in charge as you turn to Him for help will help ease your burden, both mentally and emotionally.

Life is short—a fleeting breeze. You must be intentional and diligent in each season of ministry. You must learn and grow when it is time for preparation, work hard when it is time for planting; and encourage others when it is time to equip them to do ministry. May your heart's inclination reveal that of Paul's when he said his final farewell to the Ephesian elders, "But I do not account my life of any value nor as precious to myself, if only I may finish my course and the ministry that I received from the Lord Jesus, to testify to the gospel of the grace of God" (Acts 20:24, ESV).

RETIRED PASTORS

The word "retirement" carries with it the connotation of rest or retreat from work.[13] For many church workers, retirement seems to be synonymous with an attitude of "settling down" or even "settling in" to a lifestyle with buried talents and treasures, leading to a life of meaningless monotony. And yet there is so much one can do in their retirement years—from what we always wanted to do but did not have the time, to what we can contribute to enrich the life of the church, community, family, and self.

The real issue is not what to do in retirement years but how to become motivated and ready for that season of life. Solomon's parable of the ant is wise counsel for all:

Go to the ant, you sluggard!
Consider her ways and be wise,
Which, having no captain,
Overseer or ruler,
Provides her supplies in the summer,
And gathers her food in the harvest (Prov. 6:6–8, NKJV).

For those nearing or in retirement, the winter of life is at hand! And with it will surely come the need for added provisions that are not readily obtainable if one is not working. Saving financial resources in our productive working years—during the spring, summer, and autumn seasons of life—is shrewd and logical, and, as Solomon argues, biblical: we are to be like the ants, filling up our storehouse when our strength permits it and supplies are available, in order to be prepared for the winter of our lives.

Retirement may seem to be too far into the future when we are young. But the reality is, you need to plan for your retirement at some point in your life and ministry. Here are some suggestions that may be helpful to you as you look forward to a new season.

PLAN YOUR RETIREMENT[14]

Ministers who do not plan for retirement plan to fail. Many of them get to the age of retirement only to realize they must continue to work because they need the income. Where can they go to satisfy their simple material needs after they have stopped pastoring? How can they take care of housing and related expenses for their sustenance? Should a retired pastor be dependent on his children, who may have financial challenges of their own? How can a retired pastor care for their spouse and guarantee the physical, social, and spiritual basic of life? Some countries have social security programs for their senior citizens. In some areas of the world, the church offers a retirement program. These funds may keep the elderly from indigence, but may not be enough for the comforts they had before. Hence all need a systematic savings plan in place for the care they will need during the winter season, their retirement years.

In addition to a workable savings plan, there are other areas that call for the retiree's attention and prior planning.

1. Pursue good physical health habits. Transitioning from a full-time ministry to retired life offers an opportunity for you to substantially improve your physical health. For instance, old age usually prolongs recovery from ministerial stresses and occupational disabilities that you acquired over the last few decades of ministry. However, during your transition into retirement, you have an opportunity to intentionally plan to pursue good health and prevent diseases and disabilities by choosing to change your lifestyle. A healthy retirement life is largely dependent on the choice to pursue positive lifestyle changes. These include exercise, adequate nutrition and temperance, fresh air and sunlight, hygiene and rest, and getting regular health checkups.

2. Build closer intimacy with God. When asked, "What is your greatest regret in your years of service?" most retiring pastors would say, "I didn't spend more time with God, getting to know Him more intimately." Perhaps retirement is the time to rectify that deficiency. After a lifetime focused on service, it is now time to refocus priorities and build a growing intimacy with God. Without any doubt, a minister drawing closer to retirement is more and more dependent on God, and the relationship with Him becomes more intimate. Drawing ever closer to God, letting Him lead and inspire every aspect of life. This life-stage transition often impels retirees to reassess their intimacy with God and offers a good time to build new habits for spending consistent and prolonged time with Him.

3. Cultivate new social interaction. Retirement success depends on your willingness to adapt to a lifestyle of change in your social and support networks. This is not all bad, for retention of your past lifestyle rarely results in a successful retirement. Therefore, approach your winter years with a positive attitude, and you will find new and challenging opportunities with which you can transition and pursue entirely new patterns of social support. Find new friends with whom you can share your faith, hobbies, or other interests. Get involved in activities for which you had little time while in service: regular walks with your spouse, reading refreshing books, joining a volunteer service in the community. Successful retirement almost always requires lifestyle choices that result in dramatic lifestyle changes.

4. Continue in a meaningful ministry. Retirement, a job change, and moving to a different geographical location may also alter your cognitive function and meaningful ministry. However, as a minister in retirement transition, you have the opportunity to identify new sources of cognitive stimulation and ministry—it is a lifestyle choice. For many pastors, to retire successfully simply means they retire to a different ministry, not that they give up ministry altogether. As individuals called by God, they transition to new avenues in which to serve, even with their unexpected restrictions. As they become less able to fulfill their ministerial call, they gradually transition to yet another ministry. They retire successfully and thrive cognitively because they adapt to the never-ending process of ministry transition.

PLAN FOR THE TRANSITION[15]

Although ministerial life involves many transitions, the retirement transition significantly alters life, roles, relationships, routines, and assumptions for almost all pastors. The retirement transition has more potential to alter your future—either positively or negatively—than any other life transition. Unfortunately, many pastors fritter away mental and emotional energy worrying about the changes that thrust retirement on them. Those changes may include age, loss of physical health, loss of status, loss of social prominence, or any number of other factors. While some of these changes may be beyond your control, the ability to manage the changes is in your hands. Thus it is important for you to anticipate such changes ahead of time and have a plan in reserve to handle such changes when they come your way. Do not let retirement surprise you. It is coming whether you like it or not.

Transition also reflects a psychological adjustment of attitudes and assumptions. You are the only individual who retains control over these. It will be healthier for you to process the retirement transition emotions caused by change, and choose a new, positive attitude that refocuses your energy and resources on a new lifestyle promoting your wellbeing. Letting go of the old ways can be a good thing, and inviting intentional replacements for a new lifestyle can be even better. So, welcome the change, and adventures that await you in this new phase of your life.

RETIREMENT AS SEVENTH-DAY ADVENTIST MINISTERS

Most Adventist pastors retire honorably after a long and fruitful service to the church. Usually the local congregation where they last served recognizes the pastor's lifelong ministry. That church may organize a farewell reception, to which conference leaders, previous pastors, and pastors from sister churches nearby may be invited. Appreciation for the pastor's service and the pastoral family may be expressed through appropriate speeches or reminiscing about the influence and impact the pastor has had on the congregation. Tokens of appreciation, not extravagant, are appropriate.

According to the *Church Manual*, "Retired employees deserve honor and consideration for helping build up God's church."[16] Ellen G. White also says: "The Lord would have our people understand that the pioneers in this work deserve all that our institutions can do for them. God calls upon us to understand that those who have grown old in His service deserve our love, our honor, our deepest respect."[17]

One meaningful way of expressing appreciation to the retirees is for the conference to identify possible ways of utilizing these experienced pastors to strengthen the churches and districts where such help is needed. In utilizing a retiree's services, the conference should clearly delineate the line of transition between full-time pastoral leadership and the status of retired workers—with a retiring pastor clearly instructed not to be involved in the affairs of the local congregation, and to perform only those specifically assigned ministry functions. Conflicts of ministry functions and responsibilities should be avoided.

In order to recognize the contributions retired workers have made through their leadership roles, foster appreciation and acknowledgment of their continuing service to the church, and enhance their prolonged effectiveness, the General Conference Ministerial Association makes the following specific recommendations:

- The conference or union should host a special recognition event for every honorably retired worker, clearly marking the transition from active to retiree ministry.
- Union or conference leaders should publish retirees' names in the local newsletter or official journal in appreciation of their contribution and service.
- Conference administrators may wish to continue honorary ministerial credentials, which will permit the retiree to function in various pastoral roles even after they are no longer full-time ministry employees of the denomination. Retirees should not engage in such activities unless they have been granted honorary credentials.
- Conference leaders may recruit retiree pastors on an as-needed basis to serve as preachers during pastoral interims, assistants in planning special functions, advisors in assignments where age and wisdom combine to provide good counsel, or representatives for the church in other assignments. They may also be assigned other short-term responsibilities in order to expand the evangelistic, teaching, nurture, or organizational work of the church.
- Conference leaders should instruct, and if necessary, admonish, retired workers not to attempt to control the activities of churches where they once served but which now have new pastoral leadership.

Honorary credentials. Retired church workers who are members of the Seventh-day Adventist Church in good and regular standing may receive honorary credentials, corresponding to the ones they had during active service. Credentials are granted for the duration of the conference term and must be renewed by a vote of the conference in session. The possession of out-of-date or expired credentials does not authorize a retiree to function in any of the offices of a minister. Without credentials, the retiree has no more authority or standing than any other member in the church.

The retiree's relationship to the church, as a carrier of an honorary credential, is the same as any other member, except that the church may still invite the retiree to perform baptisms, weddings, and ordinations of local leaders, especially when the church's current pastor is not available or not yet authorized to do so. In order to perform such functions, the retiree needs to make proper arrangements with the local conference or district leaders.

CONCLUSION

"There is a time for everything, and a season for every activity under the heavens" (Eccl. 3:1). No matter what season you are in now, it will eventually pass. However, as Gabrielle Blair stated, "Embrace the current season of your life." You will have seasons of joy and seasons of suffering, seasons of certainty and seasons of change, seasons of anticipation and seasons of fulfillment, seasons of youth and seasons of adulthood, seasons of fruit-bearing ministry and seasons of retirement.

Faithful Job, for whom a season of comfort and prosperity was followed by a season of darkness and despair, testified that the strength that comes from the Lord can help one plow through the highs and lows of all seasons: "The Lord gave and the Lord has taken away; may the name of the Lord be praised" (Job 1:21). Likewise Paul: "I have learned in whatever state I am, to be content: I know how to be abased, and I know how to abound. Everywhere and in all things I have learned both to be full and to be hungry, both to abound and to suffer need. I can do all things through Christ who strengthens me" (Phil. 4:11–13, NKJV).

Life through its varied seasons, indeed every day, confronts all of us with plenty of change, uncertainty, and instability, yet Scripture assures us that God's love is abundant (John 3:16) and "endures forever" (Ps. 136). Seasons come and go in our ministerial journey and in life, but Christ is "the same yesterday and today and forever" (Heb. 13:8). He gives us stability in the midst of fluidity, strength where there is weakness, direction in the face of our lostness, wisdom in times of uncertainty, and assurance in seasons of change. Without Him we cannot succeed, but with Him we cannot fail.

QUESTIONS FOR REFLECTION OR DISCUSSION

1. Why is the ministry of single pastors sensitive and misunderstood in some cultures?

2. What kind of distinctive and positive characteristics do you see in the ministry of single pastors and married pastors?

3. What counsel in the early years of your ministry would have made you a better pastor?

4. How would you define successful retirement in ministry?

5. What kind of support and involvement can the church provide to its retired pastors today, enabling them to live without fear or anxiety?

ENDNOTES

1   Chi Chi Okwu, "Pastoring While Single," http://www.smallgroups.com/articles/2016/pastoring-while-single.html?, accessed March 11, 2016.

2   *Ibid.*

3   Ellen G. White, *Steps to Christ* (Washington, DC: Review and Herald, 1956), 58.

4   This section includes information from Steve DeWitt, "Single vs. Married Pastors: Take It from a Guy Who's Been Both," March 13, 2014, https://www.thegospelcoalition.org/article/single-vs-married-pastors-take-it-from-a-guy-whos-done-both-2, accessed April 23, 2016. Used with permission.

5   White, *Gospel Workers* (Washington, DC: Review and Herald, 1915), 205.

6   This section includes information from Steve DeWitt, "Single vs. Married Pastors." Used with permission.

7   White, *Counsels to Parents, Teachers, and Students* (Mountain View, CA: Pacific Press, 1913), 99.

8   This section includes information from Joseph Mattera, "Twelve Common Mistakes Young Pastors and Leaders Make," September 2, 2012, http://www.charismanews.com/opinion/34081, accessed February 10, 2016.

9   White, *Gospel Workers*, 125.

10   *Ibid.*, 204.

11   This section includes information from Chris Adams, "Leading Through the Seasons: The Autumn of Ministry. https://womensministry.lifeway.com/2016/08/01/leading-through-the-seasons-the-autumn-of-ministry/, accessed November 13, 2016.

12   *Ibid.*

13   The information in this section is adapted from O. S. Hawkins, "Is Retirement Biblical," July 9, 2014, http://theologicalmatters.com/2014/07/09/is-retirement-biblical, accessed January 18, 2016. Used with permission.

14 This section includes information from Nathan Davis, "What is Successful Retirement for a Minister?" 2013, http://pastorselfcare.five-factor.com/? page id=948, accessed March 12, 2016. Used with permission.

15 *Ibid.*

16 *Seventh-day Adventist Church Manual*, 19th edition (Silver Spring, MD: General Conference of Seventh-day Adventists, revised 2015, updated 2016), 35.

17 White, *Gospel Workers*, 430.

CHAPTER 11

MOTIVATION FOR MINISTRY

"Our identity is not in our joy, and our identity is not in our suffering. Our identity is in Christ, whether we have joy or are suffering."—Mark Driscoll

M otivation is the driving force behind action, an incentive that propels us to keep moving forward in accomplishing a certain goal. And whether the outcome is negative, the result of a foolish desire, or positive, due to a wise endeavor, motivation thrusts us to go for it regardless. Our understanding of what we deem to be a success may be a physical desire, mental projection, materialistic aspiration, wealth acquisition, political achievement, or spiritual advancement.

In the beginning, the mirage of being like God so blinded Eve that it motivated her to disregard the will of God, and she reached out and ate the forbidden fruit. "She also gave some to her husband, who was with her, and he ate it" (Gen. 3:4–6). Adam and Eve thus plunged humanity into a disastrous destiny filled with sorrow and pain. Self-exaltation brought them down, as it did Lucifer (Isa. 14:12–15). And here we are as a result, the victims of motivation gone awry, living in the catastrophe and darkness that is sin.

When our first and foremost desire is to please our Lord and Savior, we will then be motivated to do His will and live a life that honors Him. Perhaps the best statement of positive motivation is the Christ's affirmation: " 'My food,' said Jesus, 'is to do the will of him who sent me and to finish his work' " (John 4:34). The Father willed our redemption, the eradication of sin, and the vindication of His character from Satan's accusations. From His birth to the cross, doing the will of God was Christ's delight.

As co-workers with Jesus—laboring in His ministry, taking the gospel of redemption to those who have fallen victims to sin—what is it that provides the motivation to serve? It is simple. Have you ever been in love? That special someone is ever on your mind, from the moment you first wake up in the morning to the last thought you have before falling asleep. And you go out of your way to be with that person as often as possible for as long as possible. Because of love, Jesus left the riches of heaven, bore our sorrow, and died to save us. Jesus is in love with us. We are in His mind at every moment, and He longs to be with us for eternity. He is near to all the time, standing at the door of our hearts, patiently waiting to be invited in.

As a pastor, why do you care for people, prepare sermons, preach the Word, visit hospitals, support grieving families, give counsel to distraught couples and oversee the endless tasks of church administration? Because you have fallen in love with God. And when you feel like you cannot go on any longer in ministry, why do you continue? Because you are still in love with God.

Love is the motivation, we believe, revealed by the risen Jesus in His conversation with Peter on the shores of Galilee. Three times Jesus asked Peter whether he loved Him, and three times the Master commanded Peter to feed His lambs. In that conversation is embedded the jewel of ministry's ultimate motivation. Jesus did not question Peter's faith or works. He went straight to the point: Peter faltered in his love for his Master at the moment he feared for his own safety. Now Jesus kindly ushered Peter back to his first love. It was that love for God that motivated Peter to feed His lost lambs. So it will be for us in ministry.

> The question that Christ had put to Peter was significant. He mentioned only one condition of discipleship and service. 'Lovest thou Me?' He said. This is the essential qualification. Though Peter might possess every other, yet without the love of Christ he could not be a faithful shepherd over the Lord's flock. Knowledge, benevolence, eloquence, gratitude, and zeal are all aids in the good work; but without the love of Jesus in the heart, the work of the Christian minister is a failure.[1]

Therefore, love—the love of Christ in us extended unto all who are His objects of redemption—is the ultimate and foundational motivation of ministry.

THE GREATEST MOTIVATION

Love should be our primary motivation for ministry. "For God so loved the world that he gave his only Son, that whoever believes in him shall not perish but have eternal life. For God did not send his Son into the world to condemn the world, but to save the world through him" (John 3:16, 17). God foresaw the entrance of sin and could have chosen not to create the rebellious race. Instead, He chose not to be without us. Imagine that! So He put the plan of redemption in place. And when He declared, "Let there be light!" (Gen. 1:3), He knew it would cost the life of His Son, but He created us anyway. Such is the love of our Father—a love willing to die to save sinners from sin.

It is that love of God that was manifested through Jesus, from Bethlehem as a helpless babe to His sacrifice on the cross. Love lies at the foundation of God's redemptive plan—and the motivation of gospel ministry. Only love for God enables us to uphold our calling as pastors. We have seen many pastors quit because they became bitter and resentful. Ungratefulness and false accusations destroyed their motivation. But Jesus went through that and more. The cruelty of people should cause us to have even greater love for Jesus, because we experience but a glimpse of what He went through for our sake. Being rejected by those we serve in ministry should cause His love in us to cry out, "Father, forgive them, for they do not know what they are doing" (Luke 23:34).

"Because of the increase of wickedness, the love of most will grow cold, but the one who stands firm to the end will be saved" (Matt. 24:12, 13). The one who stands firm. Stands firm in what? In love! That can only happen if God's love is in us and does not wax cold; God's love is eternal. Hence, to work as a pastor it is imperative that we fall and stay in love with the Lord! Our faithfulness is based on our relationship with Jesus, not our resources. All we do must be based on our love for Him. The Bible says that "we love [Jesus] because he first loved us" (1 John 4:19). It was His love and grace that brought me to salvation, and it is that same love and grace that enables us to live for Him and minister to and serve the lost for whom He died. "The church of Christ is organized for service. Its watchword is ministry."[2]

THE LOVE OF CHRIST IN US

To love as Christ loved energizes our work, motivates every phase of our ministry, and stimulates the exercise of every spiritual gift. Then the church, the body of Christ, will multiply and be strengthened. Paul's admonition to Christians is to "walk in love, as Christ also has loved us and given Himself for us, an offering and a sacrifice to God for a sweet-smelling aroma" (Eph. 5:2, NKJV). To walk in love is a command from which there must not be the slightest deviation by the ministers of Jesus. Christ loved us to the extent of giving Himself unreservedly for us. Likewise, we as Christians and pastors are charged to temper our ministry, prime our example, and build our fellowship with love. Any other motive for ministry is a faulty, weak excuse, and we should know that our motives will be weighed in the balance at the final judgment.

The sovereignty of love in life and Christian ministry is clearly depicted in 1 Corinthians 13. Our life and work may be as exalted as angelic praise, as convicting as a prophet who "can fathom all mysteries and all knowledge," as powerful as possessing a "faith that can move mountains," or as self-effacing as giving all we "possess to the poor" and surrender our bodies to the flames as an absolute symbol of surrender—yet these do not define ministry. For ministry to be what is delineated in Scripture, it must spring out of love. "The true Christian draws his motives of action from his deep love for his Redeemer. His affection for his Master is true and holy."[3]

Perhaps our problem in serving God with joy and unselfishness is that we love ourselves more than we love God and His people. We need to evaluate our hearts. Have we surrendered all that we are to God? How do you do that? Let us go back for a moment to that time when we fell in love. We become like putty in the presence of someone we love. What she or he determines is okay with us. All we want to do is please them. Likewise, being in love with God means we willingly become like clay in the hands of the Potter to be shaped into whatever vessel He deems we should be (Isa. 64:8). Then we serve God with joy because we have His Spirit of service within us. We express sympathy with a touch of kindness, and our words are the healing balm of Gilead. We pray for and bind the wounds of those who are suffering. Our ministry is the ministry of love.

MINISTRY BEGINS WITH LOVE

Ministry is love personified. "Love suffers long and is kind; love does not envy; love does not parade itself, is not puffed up; does not behave rudely, does not seek its own, is not provoked, thinks no evil; does not rejoice in iniquity, but rejoices in the truth; bears all things, believes all things, hopes all things, endures all things. Love never fails" (1 Cor. 13:4–8, NKJV). That unfailing love is the heart and soul of true ministry.

Without a love relationship with Jesus and His people, ministry becomes simply a job—something to do or something to get done. Unless we first experience the abiding presence of true love toward God vertically, it is impossible to be a vessel of love toward others horizontally. Only when our vertical love for God and our horizontal love for others become the true motivation for serving the Lord, can we be true recipients of God's call to ministry. Only then can we experience the call to ministry such as Peter received.

Christ mentioned to Peter only one condition of service—"Lovest thou Me?" This is the essential qualification. Though Peter might possess every other, yet without the love of Christ he could not be a faithful shepherd over the flock of God. Knowledge, benevolence, eloquence, zeal—all are essential in the good work; but without the love of Christ in the heart, the work of the Christian minister is a failure. We may have faith that visiting a shut-in will be healing to their soul, and certainly hope it will be. But love is the force that moves us to follow through with our faith and hope so that we in fact visit them. That is what the apostle Paul meant when he said, "And now these three remain: faith, hope and love. But the greatest of these is love" (1 Cor. 13:13).

The love of Christ is . . . a living principle, which is to be made manifest as an abiding power in the heart. If the character and deportment of the shepherd is an exemplification of the truth he advocates, the Lord will set the seal of His approval to the work. The shepherd and the flock will become one, united by their common hope in Christ."[4]

Hence, before you step out to answer God's call for pastoral ministry or accept any position of service in His church, reassess your love relationship with God through Jesus Christ, and your commitment of love toward those within your church and community. This reassessment should be continual, occurring again and again throughout your life and ministry.

MOTIVATION KILLERS

While proper and well-accentuated motivation is important in the fulfillment of ministry for the glory of God and the advancement of His cause on earth, it should not be forgotten that motivation can often be misguided and self-centered. On the roadmap of ministry, false or self-centered motivations often tend to divert pastors from genuine mission and soul-lifting objectives. Gospel workers should, therefore steer clear of such false motivations, some of which are discussed below.

Routines. Routines and habits are useful and essential to a successful life. Routine tends to keep order in and chaos out. Regularity and consistency are essential in the performance of specific actions. But routines can also be dangerous and deceptive if they become so repetitive that we act as if we were on autopilot. If that happens, monotony sets in and originality takes a back seat. This is especially true when we face rapid changes but, being so governed by routine, it just seems easier to continue doing what we did before. Yet, new and creative ways are in order to improve the outcome of a new challenge.

Routine makes it harder for us to step back, view the situation from a different angle to get a better perspective, and analyze how to do things differently and better. "The monotony of our service for God needs to be broken up."[5] In coming up with fresh ideas, we break out old routines that may be obsolete in certain situations. In ministry, the desire to do better, aim higher, and hope loftier should lead us to begin every morning with praise and thanksgiving.

Fear. How many times have you been defeated by fear before even attempting a task or challenge? Robert H. Schuller once said, "Better to do something imperfectly than to do nothing flawlessly." I can justify putting off just about any task by telling myself I do not have the time or resources to get it done right. The truth is, when people are afraid, they often quit. They stop taking risks. They fail to give their best effort. They stop trying. Fear keeps a pastor from moving forward. I have seen people take shot after shot and fail, until they finally hit their target. But because they did not give up, they are the most happy and successful people I know.

Church administrators can help pastors lead a life without fear by trying to understand the problems they face, lessening control and rigidity in their administrative style, and celebrating pastoral achievements. The only fear that we as Christians should have is the one the psalmist described: "The fear of the Lord is the beginning of wisdom; a good understanding have all those who do His commandments. His praise endures forever" (Ps. 111:10, NKJV).

Health issues. Health is related to motivation. Among health issues that affect a pastor's motivation in ministry are poor eating habits, lack of sufficient sleep, lack of exercise, being overworked, improper body weight, and much more. The better the pastor handles these health issues, the better his or her general health will be. A healthy life at its optimum promotes better motivation in ministry, and the pastor is able to not only enjoy personal health, but also relate to parishioners joyfully. To possess such a healthy lifestyle is challenging, especially when you want to transform many things at once. Such a transformation in life is not a simple decision, but a firm resolve for those who want to progressively adapt disciplines for lifestyle changes. "Their discipline of mind places them on vantage ground."[6] It is a process that takes time, consistency, and steady support. Once you are ready to make a change, the difficult part is committing and following through. So do your research, be aware of your health challenges, and work out a plan that will prepare you for success. Remember Paul's admonition: "Do you not know that your bodies are temples of the Holy Spirit, who is in you, whom you have received from God? You are not your own" (1 Cor. 6:19).

Pride. Repeated success can make one proud. "Pride goes before destruction" (Prov. 16:18). The wise man's caution is applicable to all areas of life, and even more so in pastoral life. If the life and ministry of a pastor are to reveal the love and grace of Jesus, can pride have a place in such a lofty ministry? Absolutely not! Therefore, I am committed to developing dynamic leadership in my ministry and church, and work hard in the various responsibilities of my ministry.

There is something wondrous in the development of ministry God has committed to all pastors. This is an area for praising God and joining the exclamation of the apostle Paul: "Therefore I glory in Christ Jesus in my service to God" (Rom. 15:17). But with success comes the enticement to take credit for oneself, and to let pride and self-glory push the pastor away from God's pathway of self-denial. When self-centeredness takes over, ministry's true intentions get derailed; the point of motivation becomes self-glory rather than God's glory. Catch a glimpse of the glory that only belong to God and learn to minister without being prideful.

Success is seductive. Pastors who have achieved it and are respected and admired are in danger of thinking that something special about themselves have earned them their highly acclaimed positions. They may shift their eyes from God to self. And if they are not vigilant, their attempts at good leadership will be derailed by pride of the heart. "Pride and the love of the world are the snares which are so great a hindrance to spirituality and a growth in grace."[7]

Failure. No one likes to fail. Whether it is at work, home, or in another area of life, failure is painful—and it can also be costly in terms of time, money, or self-worth. But failure is a normal part of life. If you never, ever suffer failure, then you are probably not pushing yourself to your full potential. It is often only through failure that we eventually meet with success.[8] Failure should be turned into an opportunity to improve one's ministry. As one strives to recover, lessons are learned and people are made stronger and wiser. But if failure is not viewed and addressed correctly, it weakens the power of motivation. "Doing nothing" may be an option, but one that will not lead to anything positive. Whatever failure you struggle with, you can learn from it and move on.

Apathy. Apathy or lack of enthusiasm for ministry erodes positive emotions that promote ministry. Pastors who lose their passion for ministry face a declining in motivation. Apathy is common and insidious and has to be confronted head-on. Pastors, at times, may experience periods of apathy when they experience a motivational dry spell. While there may not be an instant cure for apathy, we should stop to analyze what factors are causing it, and deal with them at their root. Such causative factors usually fall into one of two categories: either you do not have any set goals or your goals are unrealistic. Church administrators should consistently cast the right vision, focusing on new plans and goals, and encouraging pastors to reach a high level of enthusiasm. And although fighting apathy is not easy, under no circumstances should pastors allow apathy to overtake them to the point of bringing their laboring in ministry to a halt. There are so many reasons to feel lost and so few to get you excited. But if you focus on those few, you might find that they are more than enough to bring back your joy for ministry.

Ministry is a calling to love, care for, and serve those in the congregation of God. We are designed as God's caretakers. When we stop caring, when we cease to be earnest in ministry, we become apathetic, indifferent, and neglectful to God's calling. To minister is to actively serve. "I charge you therefore before God and the Lord Jesus Christ, who will judge the living and the dead at His appearing and His kingdom: Preach the word! Be ready in season and out of season. Convince, rebuke, exhort, with all longsuffering and teaching. . . . Be watchful in all things, endure afflictions, do the work of an evangelist, fulfill your ministry" (2 Tim. 4:1–5, NKJV). Be a minister with no room for apathy.

Burnout. Burnout is an epidemic of the modern workplace. It is the mental and physical exhaustion pastors experience when the demands of work consistently and continually exceed the amount of energy and time they have available for the performance of tasks, chores, and obligations. When pastors have no opportunity to rest, they soon loses their ability to maintain motivation. Mental and physical exhaustion may also be a sign to take some time off to rest and relax. The break need not be a two-week vacation, three-day weekend, if used for physical and mental relaxation, can be just as beneficial as long breaks from work. And during this break, they should not call the office or check email. They must let go of the routine.

Each of us is a little less important to our work than we would like to believe. In such periods of rest and relaxation, a good formula to keep in mind and practice is to "let go and let God." While tired and exhausted pastors must let go of the routine and cumbersome tasks, They must let God be their constant companion, to speak to, listen, and experience the promise: "Come to me, all you who are weary and burdened, and I will give you rest. Take my yoke upon you and learn from me, for I am gentle and humble in heart, and you will find rest for your souls" (Matt. 11:28, 29).

Lack of recognition. When pastors feel their contribution to the church is not recognized as important and effectual, the motivation to offer their best could be affected. It is important, therefore, for church administrators to recognize the importance of appreciating the work of their pastors. Appreciation and recognition are major factors in motivating employees to work harder and aim higher. Providing positive recognition of an accomplishment serves to raise individual self-esteem, reinforce their value to the organization, improve their self-image, and encourage them to accomplish even greater results in the future. Recognition is priceless, and spiritual high standing is just as important as monetary compensation. To acknowledge, therefore, a pastor's service as a blessing to the believers and to the faith community not only enhances the pastor's commitment to his calling but also augments his ministerial performance.

MOTIVATION BUILDERS

Pastors, like everyone, experience moments of discouragement especially when feeling unloved, unappreciated, and underpaid. At such times it is easy to lose motivation. The question is not whether they experience periodic lack of motivation, but how should they fight back frustration, fatigue, and apathy? And how should they recharge their fading motivation? From where does help come? For all Christians the answer is one and only one: "My help comes from the Lord, the Maker of heaven and earth" (Ps. 121:2). The following are some wholesome motivation builders for the path of ministry.

Prayer. Pray with all seriousness. Talk to God about your lack of motivation. Tell Him your tank is empty. Tell Him you have hit rock bottom. Although you may be weak, powerless, and drained of all energy, you can claim the promise: "When I am weak, then I am strong" (2 Cor. 12:10). It is not about your personal drive and motivation. It is about God's grace working in you.

The less you cherish self, the more distinct and full will be your comprehension of the excellence of your Saviour. The more closely you connect yourself with the source of light and power, the greater light will be shed upon you, and the greater power will be yours to work for God. Rejoice that you are one with God, one with Christ, and with the whole family of heaven.[9]

Friends. We are social beings; we need to have friends. In a previous chapter, we discussed how important it is for a pastor's spouse to make friends. They also play an important part in the life of a minister. Friends are an invaluable support system and enrich the life of a pastor. God uses friendships to restore sensibility and refreshment to the spirit. Pastors who do not have a trusted friend, should pray for one. For those who do, be a friend and keep in touch. "A friend loves at all times" (Prov. 17:17).

With loyal and prayer-filled friendships, pastors need not fear fading motivation. When feeling discouraged, bored, or having a midlife crisis, a friend can promote personal growth and restore or increase the motivation to overcome any crippling spiritual inertia. When I am on the slippery slope of discouragement, I take time to attend a ministry conference where I can hear life stories of other ministers with similar struggles. This reignites the fading fire in me and I gain encouragement in my own life. Sharing and praying together with other pastors helps my motivation for ministry grow. Listening to good preaching, rubbing shoulders with others in ministry, and attending focused workshops boosts my ministerial enthusiasm. And I gain new friends I can count on to be there for me, even miles away.

Lifestyle. Lifestyle and motivation are connected. Unhealthy behavior developed over time may lead to health problems or lifestyle issues that affect your ability to keep spiritual motivation high. If such is the case in your ministry, change your lifestyle. Replacing unhealthy behaviors with healthy ones requires time, discipline, and perseverance. When a new healthy behavior becomes a habit, it will be a blessing. Not only that, but one discipline leads to another. Making holistic changes takes commitment and time, but with perseverance you can do it.

Just remember that the journey may be well intentioned and well planned, but along the way there are bound to be lapses. When that happens, what is important is not to let small failures and unexpected disappointments turn into destructive tragedies. Although one mishap is just that, know that an indiscipline may also lead to another one. If you are not vigilant, you may end up worse than before (Matt. 12:43–45), because the enemy wants to crush your ministerial journey. Therefore, get back on track immediately. Hope is ahead. Grasp on to Paul's affirmation: "He [Christ] said to me, 'My grace is sufficient for you, for my power is made perfect in weakness.' Therefore I will boast all the more gladly about my weaknesses, so that Christ's power may rest on me. That is why, for Christ's sake, I delight in weaknesses, in insults, in hardships, in persecutions, in difficulties. For when I am weak, then I am strong" (2 Cor. 12:9, 10). Resolve to recover, and start again where you left off.

Bible study. "Now these things occurred as examples to keep us from setting our hearts on evil things . . . and were written down as warnings for us" (1 Cor. 10:6, 11). There is much to learn from the study of Bible characters—their failures, temptations, struggles, victories. Those whose faith made them true children of God are the best source of knowing how to fight the foe and win the battle along life's pathway of service. And the stories of those who failed to please the Lord are a stern warning of what *not* to do. As you read the Bible and identify yourself with biblical characters, you will find inspiration and motivation to overcome every disappointment, claiming victory in moments of discouragement. Read again about Noah, Jacob, Joseph, Moses, Isaiah, Jeremiah, Daniel and his friends, Nehemiah, John the Baptist, and the apostle John. Study the life of Peter, who talked like a sailor until he was converted and became a force in the preaching of the gospel; and of Paul, who persecuted the Christians, but after his conversion became a champion for truth (2 Cor. 11:23–29). The safety and success of these men of God were as much God's concern as your ministry is. Have faith, and claim victory.

In discouraging moments, remember the one who walked the path to the cross alone, and came out victorious. Meditation on the good news of Jesus Christ is a sure and certain way of having the power of His grace mediated to you. He is the cornerstone of everything we do. The motivation you need is right before you—in God's holy Word, in those God used for ministry, in the everlasting arms of our Savior:

> O how sweet to walk in this pilgrim way,
> Leaning on the everlasting arms;
> O how bright the path grows from day to day,
> Leaning on the everlasting arms.
> —Elisha A. Hoffman[10]

God. Meditate on the character of God. His glory and magnification is the goal of life and ministry. If you have lost your motivation to minister, return to God, taste and see how great and good He is, rest in His everlasting arms, and find strength in His glorious character. "The eternal God is your refuge, and underneath are the everlasting arms" (Deut. 33:27). You are serving God (Col. 3:24); find your refuge in Him. Ministry is not a performance or display of piety for people to see and applaud, nor is it a popularity contest. Ministry is about service to God. Open your Bible, God's revelation of Himself to you, and find the encouragement you have been missing.

Pastor Rick Warren says: "Motivation is contagious. I never try to motivate other people. I focus on motivating myself. When I'm motivated, I know others will catch my enthusiasm." This is true in any area of ministry. If you stay motivated, those you lead will become motivated too.

It is easy in ministry to lose sight of what we are really doing: we are serving the God of the universe, and He is working through us to change lives!

With that as the ever-sustaining focus of our ministry, nothing can distract us or destroy our motivation to follow God's calling and serve His purposes. When we are unmoved and centered in Christ crucified, risen, and coming again, then our ministry will be a powerhouse of motivation and service.

MOTIVATION FROM LOCAL CHURCH LEADERS

In a local church, the leaders are elders, deacons and deaconesses, as well as department directors, and they can do much to assist the pastor. The motivation they offer will enhance the spreading of the gospel not only by their pastor, but by all of those who come under the pastor's influence.

There are two kinds of motivation: extrinsic and intrinsic. Extrinsic motivation causes you to do something to either earn an external reward or avoid a punishment. Intrinsic motivation springs from the heart, and is not for self-interest, but rather a desire to be a blessing to others unconditionally. The former is self-centered; it makes the objective of life and all its activities focused on how to fulfill self and its consuming desires, even at the expense of using others,—including God. The latter is centered in Christ and His will for our fellow man; it rejects the priorities of self and instead places all human desire and efforts to be of service to God and neighbors.

When a pastor decisively rejects the external motivation in preference to the internal, ministry will be a remarkable and awesome blessing and privilege. But this choice is not easy. God can use local church leaders, however, to be a blessing in the pastor's life. They can offer the pastor a great encouragement by supporting them in several areas of ministry, such as follows:

Work as a team. When local church leaders stand united with the pastor and are involved in the total ministry and activities of the church, the pastor feels fully strengthened and motivated, and the ministry of the church moves forward and upward. As a result, the church as a whole becomes a center of blessings to the community and an outpost of evangelism. By total involvement in church activities and showing appreciation for the pastor's leadership, the church body works as a team with the pastor. Consequently, the pastor ministers at optimum strength, with an ongoing motivation for the growth of the church.

Be responsive. Nothing excites spiritual leaders like seeing people respond to their preaching and teaching. To note that your audience is listening to your message and responding even as you preach—perhaps by a smile, a nodding of the head, or following the Scripture references you cite—gives confidence and encouragement that your spoken word is transformed by the Holy Spirit to touch the listener. Even an occasional response of "Amen" during the sermon is a spiritual and homiletic encouragement, affirming that the preacher is firmly connected with the Word and the Spirit who inspired that Word.

When there is heart-to-heart appreciation from the congregants, when they have been deeply touched by the pastor, when a church member, pauses by the door to say thank you for the prayers and recent visit to their home, when they linger in the lobby to shake the pastor's hand in appreciation for the sermon and personal encouragement, when the youth request an intercessory prayer for a special blessing they need, or when a child just looks up and says with a smile "Hi," how could a pastor not be motivated to do the very best in ministry? A responsive congregation is a fountain of positive motivation that never dries up.

Show respect. Treating the pastor with as much respect as shown to anyone in a position of authority stimulates self-confidence and motivation in ministry. Sometimes we tend to think of the pastor as an employee of the church. That may be so, but more importantly the pastor is the spiritual leader who serves individuals and families in the congregation. Regarding King Saul, David's words are appropriate to remember: "The Lord forbid that I should do such a thing to my master, the Lord's anointed, or lay my hand on him; for he is the anointed of the Lord" (1 Sam. 24:6).

It is important for the local church elders and leaders to relate to their pastor respectfully, setting an example for the members. This brings a higher level of appreciation and understanding between pastor and parishioners. Paul's counsel is timeless: "And we urge you, brethren, to recognize those who labor among you, and are over you in the Lord and admonish you, and to esteem them very highly in love for their work's sake" (1 Thess. 5:12, 13, NKJV).

Prayer for the pastor. Church members know how much opposition they receive from the world, the flesh, and the devil, and can be assured that the pastor receives much more. Elders and all department heads should encourage members to regularly pray for their pastor. At every opportunity for group prayer, they would do well to mention the pastor's name requesting blessings for the pastoral ministry. Ask God to shower the pastor with an abundance of love, hope, joy, faith, peace, patience, power, wisdom, and courage. Pray for the pastor's maturity and growth in the faith.

Pray that God will connect them with Himself and give them wisdom, grace, and knowledge. Pray that they may be guarded from the snares of Satan and kept pure in thought and holy in heart. I entreat you who fear the Lord to waste no time in unprofitable talk or in needless labor to gratify pride or to indulge the appetite. Let the time thus gained be spent in wrestling with God for your ministers. Hold up their hands as did Aaron and Hur the hands of Moses.[11]

As Paul wrote, ministers everywhere should seek their parishioners to pray for them. "Finally, brethren, pray for us, that the word of the Lord may run swiftly and be glorified, just as it is with you, and that we may be delivered from unreasonable and wicked men; for not all have faith" (2 Thess. 3:1, 2, NKJV). A praying parish with a praying pastor assures a living, victorious church.

Avoid comparison. Local church leaders should be the first to understand that when changes occur in pastoral leadership and a new pastor takes over, they are not to compare the incoming and outgoing pastors. No two persons are alike, and no two pastors will minister in the same way. Comparisons and expectations of ministerial methods will not strengthen the new pastor's motivation. Trust God to use new spiritual leader to bring about relevant and effective ministry to meet the church's current needs. Do not stereotype the pastor either with the strengths or shortcomings of other pastors. The new pastor is not an angel dropped from heaven, but rather just a human being, with all human deficiencies and distinct personality, gifts, and talents. Pastors should serve according to their perception of the Holy Spirit's guidance. Be an enabler, and not a judge. And encourage the congregation to get to know and accept the pastor.

Be loving to the pastoral family. Do not expect the pastor or the pastoral family to be perfect. They are human too. The pastoral family has the same human strengths, deficiencies, tendencies, and drawbacks as all other families in the church. Recognizing this commonness, let the pastoral family function just like all other families in worship, fellowship, and witness. It is inappropriate to place on them a higher standard of expectations. While a pastor's family should set an exemplary model of spiritual and social life, we should not pass judgment on their life and conduct. Instead, "let us love one another, for love comes from God. Everyone who loves has been born of God and knows God. . . . God is love" (1 John 4:7, 8). Love is the great leveler of people in life and conduct; let that love be the binding relationship between the congregation and pastor's family.

Avoid criticism and gossip. As a church leader, be vigilant to muffle criticism and gossip about the pastor, for it can hurt the gospel. Ministers, as virtually all public figures, are often the subject of incessant criticism. If there is a legitimate matter that concerns the pastor, it should be addressed personally. Criticizing the pastor behind his or her back equates to hurting the anointed of the Lord; it injures the pastor's reputation and credibility, and wounds the body of Christ (see 1 Cor. 12:25–27), which is the church. All members and the pastor make up Christ's body. Therefore, it is important to avoid anything—such as slander, criticism, and gossip—that would bring dishonor to the body. Negative comments about the pastor should be met with a positive one. If misinformation is being spread, correct it with accurate information.

> Cease to dwell upon the shortcomings of others. Keep the tongue sanctified unto God. Refrain from saying anything that might detract from the influence of another; for by indulging in these words of criticism, you blaspheme God's holy name as verily as you would were you to swear.[12]

Affirm and encourage. William James, the famed psychologist, once said that the most fundamental need of human beings is appreciation. The smartest or the weakest, the most intelligent or the average, the wealthy or the poor, the skillful administrator or the failing leader, the man on the throne or the gatekeeper—each in his or her own way longs for appreciation and affirmation. So does a pastor. Appreciation is not a matter of obligation and duty but an expression of shared humanity and gratitude. Praise and appreciation do not cost anything, but they pay tremendous rewards. Even the most accomplished leaders feel encouraged by a word of appreciation and gratitude.

Local church leaders, when have you expressed gratitude to your pastor and affirmed his or her pastoral work? When was the last time you said a word of thanks for a sermon that may have touched your heart or a prayer that brought you closer to God's throne? A word of thanksgiving, a firm handshake, or a fraternal hug can do wonders in the life of your pastor. Try it.

Of course, the pastor does not stand alone. The spouse and children are also involved in the ministry of the church. Is there some way you can bring cheer to each of them so that their fellowship and ministry in your midst will continue to be a blessing? A thank you note, a birthday card, a bouquet on the pastor's anniversary, or any grateful gesture you can think of can make the pastoral family truly rejoice in the fellowship of the saints.

Are you the kind of church member who makes your pastor's ministry a joy (Heb. 13:18, 19)? Do you esteem in love the pastors whom God has placed over you (1 Thess. 5:12, 13)? Do you honor those elders who work hard at preaching and teaching (1 Tim. 5:17)? At this moment, are you walking in the truth, and thus causing your pastor to rejoice (3 John 4)? One simple way to please Christ (2 Cor. 5:9), the Head of the church (Col. 1:18), is to strive to bring joy to those whom He appoints as shepherds of His flock.

CONCLUSION

The central challenge of motivation is to give pastors a compelling reason to work enthusiastically for the church. Motivation based on the quiet yearning of the heart to glorify God by serving others will yield professional joy and fulfillment. When all is said and done, the best motivation for the pastor rests on how much the ministry is empowered by the Holy Spirit. God is the source of all strength and inspiration to pastors and church members as they consecrate themselves to serve God with humility and sacrifice. Let us not underestimate the energizing power of the Holy Spirt to move forward the gospel ministry through the work of an inspired, self-sacrificing pastor. When the single goal of the servant of God is doing His will, uplifting Jesus, and serving the flock of God unreservedly, let the congregation respond accordingly and recognize what a great blessing they are receiving in having a pastor totally committed to the work of God.

QUESTIONS FOR REFLECTION OR DISCUSSION

1. Why should love be our greatest motivation for ministry?
2. In your opinion, what are the most dangerous motivation killers?
3, What kind of motivation do we need in life and ministry? External or internal? What are the differences and challenges between the two?
4. What kind of counsel would you give to a pastor lacking proper motivation?
5. Why are feedback and appreciation from church members and leaders important in motivating pastors?

ENDNOTES

[1]   Ellen G. White, *The Desire of Ages* (Mountain View, CA: Pacific Press, 1940), 815.

[2]   White, *The Ministry of Healing* (Mountain View, CA: Pacific Press, 1942), 148.

[3]   White, *Sons and Daughters of God* (Washington, DC: Review and Herald, 1955), 288.

[4]   White, *Acts of the Apostles* (Mountain View, CA: Pacific Press, 1911), 515, 516.

[5]   White, *The Ministry of Healing*, 149.

[6]   *Ibid.*, 150.

[7]   White, *Testimonies for the Church* (Mountain View, CA: Pacific Press, 1948), 2:187.

[8]   Ali Luke, *How to Pick Yourself Up After a Failure.* An article posted online: https://www.pickthebrain.com/blog/how-to-pick-yourself-up-after-a-failure/, accessed March 12, 2016.

[9]   White, *The Desire of Ages*, 493.

[10] "Leaning on the Everlasting Arms" is a hymn published in 1887 with music by Anthony J. Showalter and lyrics by Showalter and Elisha Hoffman.

[11] White, *Testimonies for the Church*, 5:162.

[12] Ellen G. White comments in *The Seventh-day Adventist Bible Commentary* (Hagerstown, MD: Review and Herald, 1980), 5:1093.

CONCLUSION

"Change is the end result of all true learning."—Leo Buscaglia

Throughout this book, we have tried to challenge the common assumption that what we do is just another job. It is not. It is God's calling to be His spokesperson, His messenger, and a servant to His people. As a pastoral team with many years of joyful ministry, we want to leave you with some final thoughts from our ministerial experience.

[JONAS]

Ministry is a high and sacred calling. It is an invitation to unequaled privileges and challenges. It is not something for which we simply volunteer. It is the work for which we are chosen by God. The good news is that He will provide all we need to do His work in my family, in the church, and in the community—no matter how great the barriers.

I have loved every minute of being a pastor because of the opportunity ministry gives me to share God's caring love and affirm His grace with those who are hurting. To me ministry stands as a bridge that spans the gulf of separation between God and lost humanity, helping them return to Him. Is there any other experience more joyful and soul satisfying than to be involved in such a ministry? None at all. I am, therefore, convinced that being a pastor is the most fulfilling calling in life.

[RAQUEL]

Being married to a pastor has enabled me to be part of people's lives in a special way, and gives me a sense of trust and spiritual closeness with them. I love my church family, and I have been honored and humbled to be present at some of their most important moments. I have been blessed to share God's love in opportunities I might not have had if my husband had not been a pastor.

I am thankful to live in a time when what is expected from pastors' spouses is both reasonable and within our choice, and the opportunities available to us today are many. Unlike pastoral spouses of previous generations, we can choose how we serve. Some work, others continue their education, and others may be involved in various church ministries.

I also rejoice because most congregations today welcome and enable pastors' spouses to use their God-given talents. Much is given to us by way of opportunities to excel in our contributions to our spouses' ministries and be an active participant in team ministry. Thus Jonas and I are one in love, one in ministry, one in service—that is what makes a pastoral couple effective in their commitment to their church.

FINALLY . . .

"God can work miracles for His people only as they act their part with untiring energy. He calls for men of devotion to His work, men of moral courage, with ardent love for souls, and with a zeal that never flags. Such workers will find no task too arduous, no prospect too hopeless; they will labor on, undaunted, until apparent defeat is turned into glorious victory."*

Father, what a blessing it is to be a pastoral couple in Your church. We are engaged in an exalted mission of which we are not worthy. We thank You for Your call to ministry. Bless each pastoral family in a very special way, wherever they are serving You. Help us to be what you called us to be. We render You our spiritual service with joy. We thank You for that honor. In Christ's name, amen!

". . . being confident of this, that he who began a good work in you will carry it on to completion until the day of Christ Jesus."
—Philippians 1:6—

*Ellen G. White, *Prophets and Kings* (Mountain View, CA: Pacific Press, 1943), 263.